NIGHT TIMES
AND LIGHT TIMES

NIGHT TIMES
AND LIGHT TIMES
A journey through Lapland

DAVID HAY JONES

For my children, Aris and Alexandra

HAMISH HAMILTON LTD

Published by the Penguin Group
27 Wrights Lane, London W8 5TZ, England
Viking Penguin Inc, 40 West 23rd Street, New York, New York 10010, U.S.A.
Penguin Books Australia Ltd, Ringwood, Victoria, Australia
Penguin Books Canada Ltd, 2801 John Street, Markham, Ontario, Canada L3R 1B4
Penguin Books (N.Z.) Ltd, 182–190 Wairau Road, Auckland 10, New Zealand

Penguin Books Ltd, Registered Offices: Harmondsworth, Middlesex, England

First published in Great Britain 1989 by
Hamish Hamilton Ltd

Copyright © 1989 by David Hay Jones

1 3 5 7 9 10 8 6 4 2

British Library Cataloguing in Publication Data
CIP data for this book is available from the British Library

ISBN 0–241–12243 0

Printed and bound in Great Britain by
Butler & Tanner Ltd, Frome and London

Contents

List of Illustrations

Acknowledgements

Thank you to all my friends on Prestøya, Kirkenes; and Christopher Lewis, Costas Grivas, Iliana Apatzidou, Anders Sköllermo, the Kinberg family, Claes Jacobsson, Bjarte Bugge, Ann-Charlotte Åström, Bo Tage Nygren; Karl-Olof Björkman, Ella Björkman and their daughter Ella Karin.

D.H-J.

All the photographs were taken by the author.

Author's Introduction

Throughout this book I use the word Sami to describe the indigenous people of northern Scandinavia, Finland and parts of the Kola peninsula. It is the name used by the people themselves, and replaces Lapp. I use the word Samiland when referring to the region inhabited by the Sami. Although Sami and reindeer pastoralism can be found as far south as Lake Femund, my travels were in northern Samiland, above the Arctic Circle. One cannot be precise about the total numbers of Sami in Samiland but a figure of about 36,000 is often given, of which 20,000 live in Norway, 10,000 in Sweden, 4000 in Finland and 2000 in the Soviet Union. I have used the word Lapland a few times in dialogue with English-speaking people, when Samiland would mean nothing to them.

D.H-J.
Kirkenes, Norway, 1989

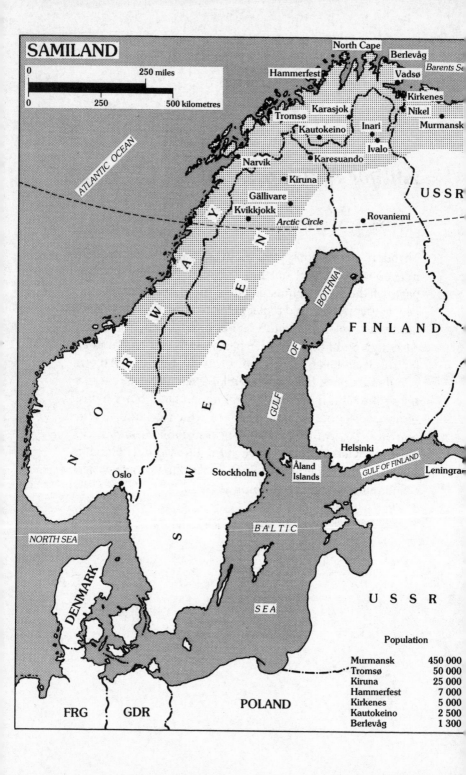

SAMILAND

0		250 miles
0	250	500 kilometres

North Cape
Berlevåg
Hammerfest
Vadsø
Barents Se
Kirkenes
Nikel
Tromsø
Karasjok
Murmansk
Kautokeino
Inari
ATLANTIC OCEAN
Ivalo
Narvik
Karesuando
USSR
Kiruna
Gällivare
Rovaniemi
Kvikkjokk
Arctic Circle

N O R W A Y

S W E D E N

BOTHNIA

FINLAND

GULF

OF

Helsinki

GULF OF FINLAND
Leningra

Oslo
Stockholm
Åland
Islands

BALTIC

NORTH SEA

DENMARK

U S S R

SEA

Population

FRG GDR POLAND

Murmansk	450 000
Tromsø	50 000
Kiruna	25 000
Hammerfest	7 000
Kirkenes	5 000
Kautokeino	2 500
Berlevåg	1 300

ONE

Piraeus: talking of leaving

There was a time when I had an office in Athens, a hotel basement near Syntagma Square. I shared it with a photographer called Angelos, from Warren, Ohio. We had a dark-room, studio, a gallery and reception area. I sat in reception and worked on a word processor. We had a sandwich bar nearby and sent Iyesha the secretary for soft drinks and rolls. We had callers six days a week: models, clients, other journalists. I sold articles to magazines in London. I gave English lessons and edited grammar books. Angelos took the pictures. It was a loose arrangement, but he had plans for expansion and partnership.

'You've got it all wrong,' Angelos told me. 'You only want to leave because you're getting trouble at home. When you're married to a Greek woman there's trouble all the time. They don't mean anything by it. And I know about your mother-in-law. Every mother-in-law is like that. Every mother even.

'You remember how I couldn't buy this place until my mother had checked it out? I told her the office is in Syntagma; five minutes away you've got the prime minister's office. She said: "Syntagma's full of tourists and tourists mean prostitutes." So she had to come, right?'

'There are prostitutes . . .' I said.

'That's not the point,' said Angelos. 'Mothers like to be involved. It's a game; you've got to play along. Doesn't mean you like it. Doesn't mean you agree. You're getting worked up for nothing. I've seen your wife. Okay, she's no beauty – most aren't – but she seems good enough to me. I can't understand why you want to leave. She's got money, hasn't she? I've seen your house. You've got more room than my father and he's been working forty years. You live by the beach. You've got two kids. What's wrong with your kids?'

'Nothing's wrong with my kids,' I said. 'I love my kids. If I could, I'd take them with me. But, like you said, Iliana's got the money. So it's best they stay with her. I don't like to say it, but it's true.'

'That boy of yours, what's his name?'

'Aris.'

'Aris, yeah. Beautiful kid, no trouble. You brought him here, what did he do? Sat on the stool and asked questions. Lovely kid.'

'Alexandra's the same. She's not even two and she cleans the house. No one asks her to. She walks around with a little brush or the hoover. She plays with cars. Aris isn't looking, she takes his cars and makes noises, driving all over the place ...'

'See, you love your kids. Running away is a stupid idea.'

'I'm not running away.'

'You're running away, man. From your family and from the business. Remember how I helped you when you were working on that shit paper for no pay? I gave you office space, said we could work something out. I figured a computer would help our image. Clients come in and see a computer, they think we're serious. You've made money too. You've sold stuff, I know.'

'The family doesn't like it. They say I'm wasting my education. The father says I should teach.'

'So what? You teach already.'

'Not full-time. He wants me to take that job in Egaleo, in the slums. I tried it for a week. The kids were okay, well behaved. When I came into the room they stood up. They asked questions. But I'm not a teacher. I don't want to be a teacher. The family should understand that.'

'That wasn't a job. Twenty hours a week. Three months' holiday. What did you have to do? Talk to a bunch of kids.'

'You try it. Boredom. Paid boredom. I told the family and they said: "Doesn't matter, it's a start. You've got to start somewhere. The kids don't see you when you're in that office till late. They miss you. Aris keeps asking for you. If you took the teaching job you could spend more time with the kids." But I know what they really want. They want to sleep all day. Iliana comes home from work at two and she wants to sleep until six. Same with her mother and father. The kids don't want to sleep, so the family expects me to look after them. I'm not stupid.'

'The trouble is, David, you don't understand the Greeks. If you live in Greece, you've got to sleep. You sleep too. I've seen you. That's why I put the bed in, so we could sleep.'

'The bed's there so you can screw the tourists with your long lens.'

'How many times have I got to tell you? You work all day down here, in the dark, without air-conditioning, you get tired. You work in that dark-room, you get a headache. So I bought the bed. So I could rest. If a tourist wants to sleep with me, that's extra, that's a bonus. That's not why I bought the bed. If I just wanted to screw I'd have bought the bed, not the gear, not the dark-room.'

'Tell that to Iliana. She saw the bed, she said: "What do you need the bed for?" I told her so we can rest. She says: "I work in a bank. I've never seen a bed in the bank. I've never seen an office with a bed."'

'What Iliana knows is that you're lazy.'

'I'm not lazy. I'm in here before you every day. I get here at nine o'clock. You're never in before twelve, never. I get up early to dress the kids and take them to nursery. Then

I have to catch the bus. I catch the bus at 7.45; takes me over an hour to get here. I've got to stand up all the way. Piraeus to Athens, all the way.'

'And you want me to do the same,' said Angelos. 'But I know about the buses, so I wait till there's no traffic, till eleven or twelve. Then I'm here till midnight. Spend most of the time answering the phone for you.'

'Iyesha answers the phone.'

'No. Iyesha goes home at four.'

'Unless she's resting in your bed. Then she leaves at midnight.'

'I spend all day in bed, how come business is so good? How come I got more work than I can handle?'

'Summer trade.'

'Okay. True. But it's only June and I'll be doing tourist pictures for another three months. Then it's portfolios and features during the winter. You were going to help. You've got the time.'

'I'm leaving.'

'I don't believe it. You're just bitching. What do you want? More space? If you want more space, take it.'

'I've got enough space. I don't need space. I'm going.'

'You don't want to leave; you can't. Every month you get problems at home. I listen to them, sort them out, then you're okay again.'

'I haven't got problems. Hell, I couldn't feel better. I'm the only one who's not worried. I'll tell you why. Three weeks ago I phoned a friend, Jimmy, in England. I've known him for years. We went to Lapland together in 1979; my first trip. I asked him, out of the blue, whether he'd like to come walking again, in the Swedish mountains. He didn't ask loads of questions, didn't say, "I'd like to, but ..." A simple "Yes". Four days later he'd arranged to take time off work. Do you know how good that feels? For the past year I've had to wait weeks at a time to talk to people, to interview them, to even get them to answer the phone.

I call a friend, a good friend, and his first word is "Yes". In a fortnight we'll be in Lapland.'

TWO

A walk in the mountains

Kvikkjokk, 50km north of the Arctic Circle, gateway to the biggest area of protected land in Europe: four national parks side by side: Rago, in Norway, 170 sq km; Padjelanta, 2010 sq km; Stora Sjöfallet, 1380 sq km: and Sareks, the wildest, 1940 sq km, with 40 peaks over 1800 metres, nearly 100 glaciers. No roads, no huts, no marked paths; often called 'the last wilderness in Europe', home of bear, wolverine, elk and lynx. It is one of the rainiest places in Sweden. In winter it is among the coldest. But in summer, temperatures are a comfortable 10 degrees or higher.

I sat on a bank of grass and tightened the laces of my Lundhags Alaska walking boots. Rubber from the ankle down, leather to within a few inches of my knees, they are the best boots I have owned. The leather is supple and strong; between walks I treat it with a dubbin mixture of fat, wax and tar. First I clean the boots with a damp rag, and when they're dry I rub in the dubbin with my fingers and keep applying it until my hand glides over the leather. Low alpine boots are no good in Samiland. They are designed for hard ground, rocks, not bog and marsh. When they get wet they stay that way. Alpine boots are unnecessarily heavy: my Lundhags are light yet give ample ankle support.

My trousers were Rohan Bags made in Milton Keynes; thin but strong, windproof and quick-drying. When packed, half a dozen pairs fit in my smallest rucksack pocket. If it's cold, I wear a pair of cotton longjohns underneath them. Around my waist I wore a black nylon belt made from the webbing used by rock climbers. Hanging from it was my Karesuando Sami knife with its short blade and rounded birchwood handle. It sits deep in the sheath so there's no danger of its falling out. I keep the blade sharp with a diamond file, a larger and finer version of the ones used for finger nails.

I also wore a cotton long-sleeved undershirt with a roll collar. Over it I had a black and red Canadian-style lumber jacket, loose fitting and warm. I had cross-country ski gloves and a mosquito hat, which covered my face, neck and ears. My face and wrists were well greased with jungle oil to keep mosquitoes at a distance.

My rucksack was a Swedish Fjällräven Gyro, a better frame model than any British or American one I had owned. It has a floating hip belt which can be adjusted easily according to terrain: uphills, downhills, flat ground. It has four big external pockets and a map case on top. There is room between the sack and the frame for a sleeping bag, tent or insulation mat.

The pack contained food for three weeks: dehydrated mostly, plus fruit juice powder, chocolate, raisins, peanuts, sardines and Russian tea. I had a Camping Gaz stove with four canisters; one change of clothing, two pairs of socks, a Caravan sleeping bag – comfortable to sleep in at minus 20° – an insulation mat, a rope and six carabiners, telescopic fishing rod, a reel with 5lb line and an assortment of flies and lures. An ice axe and walking staff were essential for fording rivers. I carried the Sareks map in my trouser pocket, and in my lumber jacket were a compass, a tube of glucose sweets and a Norwegian Helle penknife with a wooden handle and a short, pointed blade.

Jimmy was dressed like a soldier: German army parka – winter lining removed – khaki trousers, Hawkins boots with green alpine gaiters, a Puma knife on his belt. Under his mosquito hat he wore a green peaked cap which kept the gauze off his nose. He had a Karrimor sack, a Blacks sleeping bag and our Haglöfs tunnel tent.

I stood up, swinging the pack on to my back and bouncing it off my shoulders a few times. It was heavy, too heavy at 50lbs, but much of that was food, so it would get lighter. I slid my thumbs under the straps, pushed them tight across my chest and waited for Jimmy as he adjusted the hip belt of his rucksack.

He complained about the heat, said he was sweating already but didn't want to take off his parka because the pack would dig into his shoulders. It would soon be evening, I told him, and would get cooler as we climbed. He could walk as slowly as he wished; we didn't have to stay together. If he were faster, or slower, it didn't matter. The person in front would walk for half an hour then wait.

I felt strong and had no doubts about my fitness. I hate running – distance running, road running – but in the mountains with a pack I can walk all day. I keep a rough figure in mind: 5km an hour, and talk to myself as I walk, not aloud but in my head as some people read. It's a taunting kind of talk: *Go faster, go faster.* I set targets to reach, am pleased to exceed them, set others, harder each time. Walk an hour and rest, then two and rest, three and four ... I have to be in the mountains to feel like this, but I hardly notice the surroundings. It's enough to be there, to be part of the landscape, not a spectator or a tourist.

Jimmy and I walked shoulder-to-shoulder at first, along the well-trodden Kungsleden north from Kvikkjokk. The path was hard and wide, with pine boards over marshy ground. We talked breathlessly, asking questions which needed no answers: 'Steep, isn't it?'... 'Warm, isn't it?' Then Jimmy fell behind and I walked harder, my mind far from the woods, thinking of Greece and my children and how long it had been since I had felt the pleasure of walking with a pack. I thought of how, in a few years, I would take my son and daughter on trips, how we would walk on marked paths a couple of kilometres a day. Aris and Alexandra would pitch the tent and we'd collect firewood, light it at the bottom with a single match. I would show them reindeer and lemmings, teach them to spot birds and tracks.

The walking I liked; proper walking, with a map, had been one of many interests I had dropped after moving to Greece, walking only occasionally on holiday, while Iliana was resting or with Aris at our summer house near Pendeli. One day we walked to the radar station at the top, where we were stopped by soldiers and told to turn back. When Aris tired, I carried him and he fell asleep with his arm round my shoulder, his head against my neck. On the way down we stopped at a chapel and Aris crossed himself. He was only three.

In 1979 when Jimmy and I had walked from Abisko we were little more than children, enthralled by the scale of the mountains. We were frenzied, needing to move every day, and treated our route like an assault course, a test of strength and stamina. We didn't know the names of the plants we walked on or the many birds we saw. We knew only the animals, the unmistakable animals: reindeer, lynx and lemmings. There were hundreds of lemmings that year, golden and black, scurrying around the tent and rucksacks, eating our chocolate and raisins. Even a couple of years later, alone on the Kungsleden from Abisko to Kebnekaise, I was terrified most of the way. It was the first week of June with meltwater running deep and the mountainsides hard with ice. It would have been easy to ski and would have taken only three days, but like an Englishman I walked; up to my knees, up to my waist and stomach, feeling brave when I should have felt foolish.

Sounds were a comfort to me on that trip: the hissing of my gas stove, the noise of my chewing, turning the pages of a book, opening a tin of food. Sounds of what? Civilisation? Safety? The grey sky and white of the mountains seemed constant and endless. There were no comforting colours. And the wind bit my face and ears, reached in like a hand around my back and kidneys.

This time I had the confidence that comes with age, and possibly with marriage and parenthood. After London and Athens, I needed quiet and open space; no houses or roads, no parks or fields. Jimmy didn't share these views: to him, you did battle in the mountains, conquered them. Your time there was rarely enjoyable. Pleasure came later, at home when you looked back. Knowing he felt like this, I thought there might be problems if I stayed in front all the time. I had intended, or hoped, that we would alternate the lead and share decision-making. But that demanded equal fitness and the early signs were that Jimmy would continue to struggle.

When we stopped for the night, after 10km, I asked him how he was feeling.

'Fine,' he said. 'I've seen so many birds I haven't seen before. I'll have to look them up at home. And tracks. Wolverine, I think they were.'

'You don't mind walking so far apart?'

'Not if we stick to the thirty-minute rule. So long as I know what's happening.'

'You don't think we should walk together?'

'No. It's best for both of us if we stick to our own pace.'

We agreed to take it in turns to look after the map and compass, the symbols of leadership. When Jimmy was pathfinder, it didn't matter that I walked in front. If I had questions or disagreed with his route, I would wait for him to catch up and we'd sort out the problem.

The first three days took us as planned over bog and streams to the foot of Pårte, a horseshoe-shaped mountain whose southern arm overlooks Kvikkjokk, the open end facing east. It is 10km long and 15km wide. Inside, where the arms meet, is the Pårte glacier: 5km by 4.5km. From it flows Kåtokjåkkå, which joins the Rapa 12km farther east.

Our campsite below Pårte's peak gave us a view of the ground we had covered: green and flat, broken by hundreds of ponds and pools. The map showed that we had been climbing all the way, but we had hardly felt it. Pårte rose gently from its surroundings: Kvikkjokk was at 400 metres; Pårte's peak at 2000. The distance between them was 20km, in which the ground changed from dense birch wood, to marsh and treeless heath, to dwarf birch and willow, and finally the Arctic bleakness of the Pårte glacier. We were aiming for a ridge at the horseshoe's open end, where the southern arm dipped and rose to form a smaller peak called Stuor-Jerta, 1335 metres. Over the ridge, we would walk towards the glacier along Kåtokjåkkå's valley. Four kilometres from the snout, we would cut north up a valley called Jeknavagge and over the horseshoe's northern arm, skirting a 1700-metre peak, Unna Stuollo.

I felt no tireder climbing to Stuor-Jerta's ridge than I had on the flat. I walked fast, enjoying the soft crowberry surface and dwarf birch brushing my ankles. At the end of each half hour, I stopped and took a swig of water, refilling my bottle at each stream. I flushed out ptarmigan; when I was almost upon them, they flapped up and off, cackling and burring.

From the top of the ridge, I could see snow in the distance, on level ground before the slope down to Kåtok-jåkkå valley. I aimed for it and when I reached the edge, where the snow was soft and grey, stopped to wait for Jimmy. I stepped on to the snow to see whether it would hold my weight. About five metres in it was firm, crunching underfoot, a better walking surface than the rocks around it. Among some green-stained stones I saw glacier buttercups, the only flower that grows above 2000 metres in Sweden.

Jimmy staggered red-faced into view and dumped his pack next to mine. Pointing at the snow, he said: 'This must be worth a long rest.'

I passed him my water bottle.

'There's no more climbing today,' he said and tossed me the map. 'From here we descend to a cottage and a bridge beyond it. I reckon we can cross the bridge and camp where Jeknavagge meets Kåtok.'

I measured the distance with the ruler on my compass. 'Six kilometres,' I said. 'We'll be there in an hour and a half.'

'Call it two,' said Jimmy.

I passed the map back. He studied it, sitting on his rucksack, his boot heels in snow. 'Have you noticed,' he said, 'all these Sami words describe places.'

The map had a glossary of Sami words next to the key and I had written some more on the back.

'I know some of them,' I said. 'Check these: *jaure* means lake; *tjåkkå*, that's peak; *suoloi* is an island; *vare* is a mountain; *jegge* is a bog; *stuor*, that's big; *unna* means little. How am I doing?'

'Not bad. There are plenty more.'

'There are words which cannot be translated into English because they describe features we don't see. To us, it's just mountain and bog.'

'And most of it's a pain in the arse. Still, it's nice to know that people have lived here. Comforting.'

'They still do,' I said. 'For part of the year, during the summer, with their reindeer. Sami has hundreds of words which describe reindeer: their size and sex and shape, the way they move, the sounds they make.'

'Yeah, and I've got just as many to describe mosquitoes. Do you want to hear them?'

'I've heard them.'

We walked side by side to the hut, stopped there a few minutes, then walked on to the bridge – a narrow, cable structure which swayed under our feet. Below roared the Kåtok river, hissing and spitting as it cut a line through the blue-grey rock. After the bridge we were on firm snow for 200 metres, then on scree to our campsite.

We pitched the tent on soggy moss and held the guy ropes down with rocks. Jimmy unpacked his sleeping bag and insulation mat and tossed them into the tent. He watched me pull my water bottle from its pocket and unclip my stove and pots.

'What are you doing?' he asked.

'Making dinner.'

'Not for my sake,' he said.

'Aren't you hungry?'

'No. I want to sleep.'

'Thirsty? How about some tea?'

'I'm not thirsty,' he said, crawled into the tent and zipped down the inner flaps. 'Close the flysheet,' he shouted. I zipped it down and put a rock over the material to stop it flapping.

I sat by my rucksack, irked by Jimmy's sudden change of mood. What was bothering him? I thought the day had gone well, that he would be pleased to have reached the mountains, glad to see ice and rock after so many kilometres on marshland. For me the good days were about to begin; I hoped Jimmy wouldn't spoil them.

In the morning, Jimmy was quiet. He didn't want to talk. He didn't want to eat. His first words were: 'Let's get a move on.'

'We need breakfast,' I said. 'Even if it's just a cup of tea, a piece of chocolate.'

'I'm all right. I'm not hungry.'

'What's up, Jim?'

'Nothing. I'm not keen, that's all. Look at this place. It's horrible. And you can't hear anything. The river's so loud.'

'Do you want to turn back?' I asked.

'I'm not backing out,' he snapped. 'I'm just not keen.'

'Look at the map,' I said. 'From here to Unna Stuollo won't be a problem. We climb 300 metres in 5km. That's nothing. It won't take more than a couple of hours, and most of it will be on hard snow. At Unna Stuollo there are two ridges, one on each side of the summit. We take the east ridge, a climb of 300 metres in 1.5km; steep but not difficult. Snow all the way, and at the top we'll be on flat ground for 2km. After that, there's a steep descent, snow then vegetation, and birch wood at Rapa. Total distance, 12 km. Shouldn't take more than ten hours non-stop.'

'What about the weather?'

'It'll hold. Look at the sky. Doesn't look like rain. We'll be fine, and if it breaks, we stop and wait. No risks.'

Jimmy walked in front, picking out a route on the loose rock of Jeknavagge's east slope. We walked high above the stream, which was barely visible to our left. We passed boulders, some two metres high, and in places crossed flat thin stones which rocked when we stepped on them. Some were wet and slimy and threw us off balance. We rock-hopped over boulder fields, half falling from boulder to boulder, not quite in control, kept upright by momentum.

In one resting place, as we were leaning against a boulder, we heard rumbling and the click, click of rocks rolling down a hillside. 'Avalanche,' said Jimmy and we stood to look ... not an avalanche but a herd of reindeer, 30 metres above, making its way slowly along the valley side. We watched their graceful progress over the unstable ground. One stopped, held his head high and sniffed the air. Our eyes met and he stared and then snorted to alert the others. They panicked momentarily, began to scatter, but order soon returned and they trotted in a group towards the peaks ahead of us.

'What are they doing up here?' asked Jimmy.

'It's cool,' I said. 'No flies or mosquitoes.'

At the southern end of Unna Stuollo, at the point where we would begin our ascent, we crossed a small frozen lake, not knowing it was a lake until we saw its dark green ice in the middle and the crack patterns deep below. For the next six hours we would be on snow and ice all the way.

I unpacked my ice axe and mittens and put on my black woollen hat, pulling it down over my ears. I led and climbed eagerly, quickly, in a straight line, straying from it only where there were patches of refrozen ice and my boots wouldn't grip. When I rested, I stood on my boot tips and leant forward with both hands over my ice axe, its shaft pressed deep into the snow. The higher we climbed, the harder it became to kick steps, to make an impression on the icy surface. Sometimes I slipped but was kept from falling by the axe's wrist strap; hair and face full of snow, I lay for a few seconds, then pressed up on to my knees and feet.

I suggested that Jimmy should lead: he was heavier and might find it easier to kick his way. We tried for 50 metres but his progress was so slow that I had to wait shivering while he kicked and hacked. He turned and snarled: 'Fuck off out of the way.'

I skirted him and pressed on, kicking hard to build a lead. Approaching halfway, I was in pain, breathing deep into my chest, and had to stop every few steps, gasping, sucking, afraid I might have to give up. I no longer lifted my legs but dragged them feebly over the snow. Each breath was a step, an audible 'huh'. My thighs felt dead; my ankles were stiff, my calfs locked tight. I felt miserable, angry at my failing strength. I tried desperately to push on, to forget the pain and walk, but could find nothing.

I looked around expecting to see Jimmy on my shoulder but he was more than 100 metres below. I rested and watched his almost arthritic progress. He walked three steps at a time and then slumped over his ice axe, falling to his knees and elbows. I had to keep going, for both of us. If I weakened or worried, it would give Jimmy more reason to complain and insist we turn back. If he could manage three steps, I would walk five and stop, six and stop, seven, eight... Mind empty except for those numbers, I climbed. Each step a breath, a number and at the end a rest. Push back the pain, the shaking, and keep on. Nearing the top, grunting, forcing air in and out... 344, 345, 346, 347, a few more steps, 348, 349, 350, top here, 351. I dropped to my knees, pulled the pack off and rolled on to my back, felt icy water seeping through my trousers and vest. I closed my eyes, so grateful that the pain had ended.

Where was Jimmy? I looked down between my legs but couldn't see him. I looked at my watch and then slept and waited ... footsteps approaching ... fifteen minutes had passed. I saw Jimmy's head, then his chest and knees. He wasn't walking; he was shuffling, staggering towards me. And when he drew level, he stood breathless, not speaking. He threw his ice axe on to the snow, so close to my feet that I had to lift my legs to avoid being hit.

'Careful,' I said.

'I'm dead.'

'Hard work, eh?'

'Stupid,' he said. He took off his pack, sat on it and wiped his ice axe dry with his mittens. 'How come you were so far ahead?' he said. 'The agreement was to rest every half hour. You walked for more than an hour.'

'I didn't think it mattered here.'

'I didn't know where the hell you were. You know what that feels like?'

'I'm sorry. I was in pain too.'

'Didn't look like it.'

I took a bar of chocolate out of my pocket. 'Want some?'

'I want to go home,' he said. 'I've had enough.'

I didn't answer.

'I think we should head straight for Suorva,' he said. 'Forget Sarek.'

No point in arguing. Whichever route we took there would be problems ahead. Our descent to Rapa was on steeper ground than the climb to Unna Stuollo; it would be another four or five hours before we could camp.

After the 2km stretch of flat ground, we reached the valley rim where the climb down would begin.

'Looks bloody steep,' said Jimmy. 'The ground seems to disappear.'

'It'll look better from the edge,' I said. 'We can't see what's below us yet.'

We inched our way forward and had what looked like a ski jump below.

'Christ,' said Jimmy. 'If we fall here we won't stop till we reach the river. How far is it?'

'About 400 metres.'

'Sod that. Isn't there another way down?'

'No. This is the easiest way.'

'You prat, Jones. Don't you ever look at the map?' Jimmy walked forward a couple of steps, stood with hands on hips looking at the drop. 'Mad,' he said.

'It's not difficult, Jim.'

'It's dangerous,' he said.

'I'll go first.'

'Too right you will.'

I zig-zagged down to a ledge, tentative steps for the first few metres and then I ran, doing jump turns like an alpine skier. Below was an even steeper slope and choice of routes: on snow or rock. 'Which do you want?' I asked.

'God knows,' said Jimmy.

'I'll stick to the snow.' I descended 30 metres. Fear stopped me. The snow was at avalanche angle. When I stepped, the crust loosened and slid in seat-sized sheets down the slope. Walking in any direction was dangerous. Least risk? I headed for the line where snow met rock.

I tested each step, making sure the snow was stable.

Before transferring weight from one foot to another, I drove my axe in deep, hoping it would hold if I fell.

I should have known that something was wrong when I heard balls of snow bouncing down the slope behind me. I should have known that Jimmy was in trouble, but all that mattered was saving myself. Slowly, steadily I stepped towards the rocks and relative safety. Behind me blocks of snow were sliding down like a moving staircase ... I looked up at Jimmy, 30 metres away. He was moving too fast, trying to run as I had been doing earlier, but here the slope was dangerously steep. Shouting, I knew, wouldn't help and might move the snow above him. So I waited and watched. *Jimmy should know better*, I thought. *He should know that the snow won't hold.*

A big sheet of ice slid out from under him, breaking into sharp-edged pieces which rolled down, picking up speed and hurtling past me. Jimmy was still on his feet but sliding down, and all around him the surface was cracking and creeping. I didn't look at his face; kept my eyes locked on his feet. Why didn't he do something?

An image, a memory, came to me: winter in Coniston; I was on the way down from a gulley climb, 50 metres from the valley floor. I was running, I tripped, was sent flying into the air and landed on my chest. I tore down the mountain head first. Somewhere in the fall I'd dropped my ice axe, had nothing to brake with ...

'Drop on your axe,' I shouted.

He kept sliding, then suddenly and clumsily dropped into a sitting position, spun around so that he was falling sideways. He rolled on to his stomach, then his back, head first down the slope. The edge was coming, and beyond it ...? Somehow his axe tip gripped, caught the snow and swung him round. He was on his stomach, pressing down on the axe, legs wide apart, braking, cutting across the snow tongue, heading for the rocks some metres below me. He hit them and bounced, bounced again, and was thrown onto his back so the rucksack snagged, and he lay there like a beetle, legs kicking in the air. Then he rolled on to his side and lay still.

I dumped my pack and charged down. Was he hurt? Had he broken a leg? Was he conscious? I saw him move on to his stomach and struggle out of his pack. He knelt and looked up – smiling, laughing.

'Are you all right?' I shouted.

He kept smiling, stupidly, thrusting his right arm into the air.

'Are you okay, Jim?'

'I made it,' he whooped. 'I fucking made it.'

'Are you okay? Nothing broken?'

He was crying; smiling and crying at the same time. The sobs kept him from talking. I thumped him on the back.

'Well done, mate.'

'I made it,' he said.

I sat and looked at him, wondering what would come next: more tears, pain, disbelief? 'Are you all right, Jim?'

'I think so.'

'Can you move your legs, your arms?'

'Yeah. I don't think I've broken anything.' He opened and closed his hands, testing the fingers. 'Did you see that?' he said. 'It felt like 100 miles an hour.'

'You did well.'

'I didn't know what I was doing. I saw the rocks coming and thought that was it.'

'Your rucksack helped.'

'Not on the snow it didn't. The bloody thing kept pulling me around ...'

I walked back up the slope to fetch my pack and, looking at the path of his fall, guessed he had fallen 40 or 50 metres.

'Look at my hands,' he said when I rejoined him. 'I've got the shakes. I still don't believe I made it.'

'You did.'

'I could have died, Dave.' I left that unanswered. 'That's it,' said Jimmy.

'What?'

'No more. We're going home now.'

'Yeah. We're going home.'

We had two more hours of walking ahead, much of it on the kind of snow and slope where Jimmy had fallen. The snow tongues were 30 metres wide, separated by fingers of rocky ground. Every step seemed a stupid, careless risk, but I was enjoying it – the sour, dry taste in my mouth, the adrenalin pumping.

More and more of the Rapa valley was revealed as we descended, and thirty minutes from the bottom we were on soft, safe crowberry where falling didn't matter. Lower down we were among tiny twisted birch trees and I stopped to take pictures.

'Valley of the beasts,' I said pointing to where the Rapa was joined by a smaller river, Sarvesjåkkå.

'Yeah,' said Jimmy. 'I'll meet you down there. See that gravel bank by the river? I'll pitch the tent on the flat ground nearest to that.'

I shot half a roll using my wide-angle lens, then fitted the telephoto to get a closer view of the Rapa and the next day's walk. It wouldn't be easy, I saw. The river was deep and wide. We'd have to spend most of the day picking our way from island to island, using the ropes if necessary, wet the whole day. It remained to be seen how Jimmy would react.

I loaded a fresh film and walked to meet him, descending through birch trees and grass to a clearing above the gravel bank. Jimmy had pitched the tent and was shaking his sleeping bag. 'Getting some fresh air into it,' he said.

'Do you want to eat?'

'I want to be left alone for a while.'

I dumped my pack against a birch stump, pulled out my

sleeping bag and crawled into the tent. No food, no drink. Nothing more said to Jimmy that day.

Later, close to midnight, I woke and lay thinking of what had happened during the past few days, trying to find where Jimmy and I had stopped needing each other's company. The mountains, through some strange power which I didn't like or understand, were pushing me to be rid of him. If he had fallen those 400 metres to the valley floor, I wouldn't have been upset. I knew where my thoughts were leading and, knowing they were wrong, I left the tent and walked to the riverside. I sat under a birch tree on the damp grass and let my gaze drift to the nearby flowers. I didn't know their English names, only the Latin: Saxifrage, Potentilla, Astralagus, Viola, Cassiope.

I looked up, hoping to see a lynx or wolverine or reindeer; nothing. So I listened: loudest was the wind, and under it the tumbling of water. There was my breathing and the blood surging through my temples. In a few days I would be alone and these sounds, of landscape and my body, would keep me company. It was a long time to wait, too long. I wanted to be alone now. I could pack while Jimmy slept, slide my sleeping bag and mat out of the tent. I'd leave him some food but take the stove. He could keep the map and compass. I knew my way through Sareks. His company was too much of a burden. His depressions were so unpredictable that I didn't know whether it was safe to talk to him. He had a temper, and could be violent if pushed. How much longer could we go on scraping each other's nerves? If I left, Jimmy would be able to concentrate his energy. *I* was getting him down, not the weather, not the terrain. Perhaps, on his own, he would learn to like Sareks.

I crept towards the tent, my footsteps hidden by the wind. At the entrance I knelt and, holding the flysheet with my left hand, zipped up with the right. Gently, mil-

limetres at a time; mustn't wake him. Now the inner tent.
Jimmy's head was inches away ...

'What the fuck are you playing at?' he shouted. 'Come
in if you want to come in.'

I looked inside. 'Did you hear me?' I asked.

'Not until you were pissing around with the zip.'

'I was trying not to wake you. I thought I was quiet.'

'You weren't when you got to the tent. I heard you.'

'I'm sorry.'

'Okay. Why don't you sleep? We've got a tough day
tomorrow.'

'Right.'

Late morning. The night hours forgotten. A river to cross...
We walked over gravel and high grass to the first channel
and waded through shallow silty water to an island. We
crossed the island's willow scrub and waded another
stream, skirted a second island and crossed a 10-metre
wide channel where the current was strong.

We worked this way for nearly an hour; over streams
and islands, zig-zagging our way across, walking west,
doubling back, dumping our packs to study the options.
The best place to cross channels, we found, was where
they split in two, dividing their strength and volume, rip-
pling over the shingle below. Where the channels widened
and deepened, we took it in turns to lead. Jimmy took the
first, probing with his feet, not putting them down until he
knew the stones below would hold, keeping at least two
points of contact with the bed: both feet, or a foot and his
staff. We waded up to our waists, having to fight our way
forward, feeling the river push our legs aside as we stepped.
Twice we turned back, not wanting to go in over our
stomachs, afraid that the flow might tip and dump us.

We reached the last channel, 15 metres from the
opposite bank and our quick route to Suorva.

'Looks bad,' said Jimmy.

'It's not fast,' I said.

'It's deep though.'

The water wasn't glacial green but muddy. The river had torn at its banks and even as we stood, in those few minutes, we saw lumps of peat and mud drop into the water and sink from view. 'We've got to try,' I said.

'You sure it's worth it?'

'We'll soon see.'

Five metres out, I was up to my stomach, searching for solid ground with the soles of my boots. I was neither tall enough nor strong enough to cut straight across. I headed diagonally, using the current to help me, letting it push me forward. Jimmy was shouting advice, but I couldn't make out the words, couldn't turn to speak, couldn't move forwards, sideways or back. My legs were shaking. The water was pressing, pushing me off balance. I unhooked one arm of my rucksack so that I could free myself if dragged under.

How could I get to where Jimmy was standing? Walking backwards was impossible. And if I turned to face the current it would knock me off my feet ... I stood my ground, unable, unwilling to move.

'Do you want the rope?' shouted Jimmy. I didn't reply. How could the problem be solved? And quickly? The staff could not take much more: it was already bowing and quivering. I had to use the current, couldn't fight against it. I shuffled backwards diagonally, leading with my right leg, staff out in front, left leg last to move. I kept as thin a profile as I could: my left side and the side of my rucksack facing the flow.

Out of danger. In all, a second or so of panic, ten minutes of fear, and then relief, knowing I wouldn't fall. Drenched from my chest down, I waded towards Jimmy.

'Do you want to try it?' I asked.

'Get stuffed. We'll go back and cross Sarvesjåkkå. There's a bridge 13 km north of here.'

Out of the water, my cockiness returned. 'Wasn't that bad. I nearly made it.'

'Nowhere near it,' sneered Jimmy.

'Five metres. That's all.'

'Might as well have been a mile.'

The complaints were like needle jabs: petty, picking. 'Stop moaning, for Christ's sake,' I shouted.

'It was your stupid idea to try crossing.'

'At least I tried.'

'What a hero.'

'Shit, Jim. What is it with you?'

'I hate it here,' he said. 'It's not even good to look at.'

I wanted to scream at him, hit him. 'What do you want, for God's sake?'

'You said we'd see animals. We haven't seen any.'

'You spend all your time sleeping, what do you expect?'

'That's because I'm knackered trying to keep up with you. This isn't the kind of walking I wanted.'

I was on the verge of swinging my axe at his head.

'What did you want? A Sunday afternoon stroll?'

'You said we'd be able to paddle across that river. Look at it. You couldn't even row across.'

'That's the point,' I shouted. 'That's the bloody point. I don't have the answers. I didn't know what it was going to be like. That's why I'm here.'

'You haven't got a clue what you're doing.'

'Just shut it, Jim. Let's walk.'

'Now you're talking sense.'

We walked north, through bog and streams, through birch wood and dripping willow. We didn't stop to change clothes or rest. Whenever I felt Jimmy was too close, I walked faster, pushing him to complain, to say stop. We agreed on one thing: our goal for the day was the bridge. It was all that mattered. For Jimmy, reaching it meant a day closer to home. For me, it meant only two days to go, then I would be alone.

Eight kilometres from Sarvesjåkkå, the Rapa widened, spreading its flow around an expanse of silt flats. It looked temptingly easy to cross, but the bridge was such a fixed idea that we dared not speak about crossing anywhere else.

Our path took us close to the river, so close that we could see there was no strength in it. I picked out possible routes, from silt flat to silt flat. The idea was gaining strength, but I didn't voice it. I saw Jimmy was thinking the same; we slowed, studying the possibilities. If only we could cross here: we'd save half a day. It had to be worth a try. Should I say something?

Jimmy spoke: 'I think we can do it.'

'Yeah?'

'Look. We start at that silt flat closest to the bank, cross it; there's a narrow channel from there to the next. We cross that and there's another channel. Look at it. Can't be more than knee-deep.'

'And from there?'

'It's obvious. Can't you see the route? From flat to flat. There's no deep water.'

'Okay. We'll try it.'

The route was so easy a child could have paddled across. At its deepest, the water reached our knees and with so little force that we splashed across without worrying about tripping or falling. Jimmy rushed for the bank and when he reached it thrust his arm into the air, just as he'd done when he'd fallen on the ice. He held out his hand, pulled me up on to the bank. We hugged.

'We've bloody made it, Dave.'

'Yeah, we've cracked it now.'

'We're out; we're on our way home.'

The animosity which had been building up, the hatred pushing me to hit Jimmy, disappeared; dispersed so quickly that I hardly believed how violent my intentions had been an hour before. I had disliked Jimmy for not being able to cope, for talking about home when his mind should have been on the mountains. But my reaction had been just as disturbed: my belief that I understood the mountains was so far from the truth that I cringed at the thought of it.

In the morning, after a tense but welcome meal, we began to talk as friends and to listen to each other. I even slowed and chatted with Jimmy as we walked, admitting bit by bit how frightened, how tired, how close to giving up I had been.

'I couldn't have done it without you, Dave.'

'I was a shit,' I said. 'I'm sorry.'

Next day we were in Suorva waiting for the bus to Gällivare. Jimmy wanted to stay there a couple of days, to rest, to wash and shave before catching the plane to Stockholm and London.

He had stopped talking about our walk, said that his girlfriend would pick him up at Heathrow, where they'd spend a night at an hotel before driving home to Droitwich. He looked forward to drinking at his local pub, to Indian food, to his bed, to sex.

'What are your plans, Dave?' he asked.

'I haven't had enough yet,' I said. 'I'll carry on to Kebnekaise, stock up with food at the mountain station, keep walking while the weather's good.'

I was ready to carry on alone. Jimmy's company had helped, had broken me in slowly. I was no longer afraid of the mountains or the weather or loneliness.

THREE

Sami questions

Kebnekaise, 2117 metres above sea level, is Sweden's highest mountain. It is neither as imposing nor as hard to climb as the many smaller peaks in Sarek and across the border in Norway, but to Swedes it is important, just as Ben Nevis is to the British.

The first mountain station was built by the Swedish Tourist Federation, STF, in 1908 and could accommodate ten men and eight women. Since then it has been rebuilt and added to many times. Today it resembles an hotel, with a restaurant, food shop, sauna and showers. It is a base for mountain walking and skiing, both Nordic and *haute route*. Throughout the summer season, from June to September, the STF organises guided walks to the glacial summit of Kebnekaise, following the so-called East route which takes most of a day, there and back. It is not a technically difficult climb; I saw people on the summit in wellington boots; there were children who had not yet reached their teens and men and women past retirement age.

In the mountain station's library I read that 50,000 people pass Kebnekaise each year. The author was enthusiastic about so many people receiving 'a mountain education'. The figure frightened me. Fifty thousand; that's as big as a town. I thought of the damage done to plants and wildlife, to grazing reindeer. I thought of the facilities people would demand to make their future walks comfortable:

shops, huts, kitchens with electric cookers; that horrible idea – self-catering holidays.

One morning, an intensely bright and warm day, I heard a helicopter approaching. Within minutes it had reached the main building and was preparing to land, 20 metres in front of me. I had to hold my hands over my ears to muffle the roaring and whining of the engine and rotor blades. A couple of people joined me. We stood in a line looking at the helicopter. At first I thought it might have come to fly some climbers to hospital: perhaps they had fallen down a crevasse. But the man next to me said: 'Ridiculous, isn't it?'

'What?'

'The helicopter, people coming to the mountains by helicopter.'

'Where does it come from?' I asked.

'Nikkaluokta.'

'But that's only a day away, 20km.'

'I know. People are lazy.'

We introduced ourselves, shook hands: his name was Claes; he lived in Gällivare, was born and brought up there, but had also lived in Kiruna, Stockholm and Skara. He was interested that an Englishman should come to Sweden to walk: 'You've got Scotland,' he said. 'Why come here?'

I told him I had been coming to Samiland for eight years, that it was one of those places you keep coming back to.

'I know what you mean,' he said.'I come to the mountains whenever I can. I have been walking here for more than twenty years: Kebnekaise, Sarek, the Arjeplog mountains, Treriksröset. I've climbed in Norway too: Sulitjelma, Saltfjellet, Bjørnfjellet. I like Kebnekaise best. Sometimes I wonder why. The changes have been frightening.'

'Such as?'

'Look at Abisko National Park, north of here, or Stora Sjöfallet, farther south, near Sarek. You can't call them national parks any more. A national park is supposed to preserve an area in its natural state or let it evolve naturally. You've got a road right through Abisko, the one to Narvik. It follows the railway line, so what do we need it for?'

'For the tourists, for the people who live in Kiruna.'

'Exactly. Abisko has become a ski resort. There are ski lifts, a supermarket, a petrol station. The road attracts a lot of people who couldn't care less about the mountains, and it pushes out the serious walkers. They go to Sarek now, or they walk north of Torneträsk, which disturbs those areas.'

'I've heard that the Kiruna mountains are going to be made into a national park, Sweden's biggest.'

'That's right. The problem is that there are so many pressure groups who want a say, who want exemption from national park rules. Hunters want to be able to shoot elk, fishermen want their competitions and fishing huts. The Sami don't want the reindeers' natural enemies to be protected: wolverine, lynx and wolves, if there are any.'

'I've seen Stora Sjöfallet,' I said, 'a couple of weeks ago.'

'Stora Sjöfallet is a tragedy. It was the biggest waterfall in northern Europe. Now it's a power station. The character of the place has changed completely, a landscape that had existed for thousands of years, which the Sami and their reindeer had got used to. You can't change a reindeer's habits easily. Build a road across a migration route, or drown grazing land, and it takes generations before the animals will use other routes, other grazing areas. What happens? People give up reindeer pastoralism. Do you remember Alta?'

'The conflict? In the early eighties.'

'That's right. The Norwegian authorities proposed a scheme which would have flooded not only grazing land but a Sami village, Masi. That was in the late sixties. Masi was one of the few purely Sami villages in Norway – a couple of hundred people lived there, which is a lot

considering there are only 20,000 Sami in Norway. That
the state could have proposed such a scheme shows it
doesn't understand or care about outlying areas, the
mountains and *vidda*. Imagine the arrogance behind it:
being ready to take away the livelihoods of hundreds of
people, destroy a village which was not only economically
important but ... spiritually, if you like, culturally.'

'But Masi was saved.'

'Of course it was. The government had to give in because
of the protests. The scheme which was accepted, the one
which was built, was much smaller. A lot of land was
saved but that doesn't mean that the state understood
the Sami argument. People have little idea how complex
reindeer pastoralism is. When engineers propose building
a road or a dam, they say a certain number of hectares
will be affected – the area of the road. But the impact of
construction goes beyond those few hectares. It can upset
the flow of deer.'

'How?'

'Reindeer aren't like cows. They don't stay in one place,
in a field. They migrate, between the interior and the
coast, between the forest and the mountains. Thousands of
animals owned by different families, each with its own
migration route. Different groups of animals can occupy
the same space but at slightly different times. If a road is
built, it can push a herd on to another route so that animals
become mixed, so that land is overgrazed. It can cause
bottlenecks. Norwegian hydro didn't take that into
account.'

'Or ignored it. I remember the demonstrations. I was
living in Denmark at the time. Alta was on the news a lot,
on television; 1981, it must have been.

'The winter of '81, yes. A thousand demonstrators from
all over the world, hundreds of police. The demonstrators
chained themselves together and had to be cut free. Everyone was fined. I'll tell you something else. The woman who

is now prime minister of Norway, Gro Harlem Brundtland, took over as prime minister then. There were Sami hunger strikes in Oslo at the same time as she came to power. Previously she had been environment minister, had agreed with the Alta scheme. Now, for some reason, the world thinks she's a great campaigner for protection of the environment. In 1981 she didn't care about the Sami and probably still doesn't.'

I had nothing to add to that. Mrs Harlem Brundtland has more to think about than the Sami. The people she represents, four million Norwegians, belong to industrial Europe which needs power, raw materials, cars and roads, resorts.

The 20,000 Norwegian Sami are an inconvenience. In industrial countries, people are supposed to live in towns where they can be provided with electricity, running water, jobs, unemployment benefit, paid holidays, restaurants. Even farmers stay in one place. But the Sami wander, and the land they need must be unspoilt, untouched by industry. In Europe – even in tolerant Scandinavia – this is considered backward.

Wherever possible, the Nordic countries have made the Sami Norwegian, Swedish, Finnish. The reindeer Sami, always a minority, have survived because they live as no Scandinavian would want to. On the coast of Norway, where they were fishermen, they have all but disappeared as a distinct group. Waves of Norwegian and Finnish colonisation, industrial fishing and nationalistic government action have wiped out sea Sami culture and language. Though the details are different, the same has happened to the forest Sami of Sweden, the river Sami of Norway, the semi-nomadic Skolt Sami in Finland. And the Soviet Union, which collectivised reindeer pastoralism shortly after the revolution, has, by one negligent act, done more than any other country to harm the Sami way of life: Chernobyl. I asked Claes about its effects in Scandinavia.

'Where I live, northern Sweden, wasn't affected, but central Sweden and Norway received heavy fall-out, in a belt between Gävle and Umeå, right across the country.'

'Southern Samiland.'

'Yes. The Sami were hard hit because reindeer eat lichen which absorbs radioactive substances. Their meat became contaminated with caesium, was unfit for consumption. Fish in mountain lakes were also affected, exceeding the 300bq limit set by the government.'

'What happened to the reindeer which couldn't be eaten?'

'The government bought them. They were fed to mink. But the problems will persist for years. Even though the reindeer meat you can buy in shops is perfectly safe, people are reluctant to buy it – it has a bad reputation now. So Chernobyl has affected all Sami, even those in the far north.'

'And compensation doesn't help if you know that your herds will be unfit to sell and eat.'

'No, it doesn't. There's no longer a reason for carrying on.'

Despite this, I was sure the Sami would survive. Just as you can't force reindeer to change the habits of hundreds of years, you can't make the Sami give up a way of life that is theirs: they are the reindeer people. Out of pride, out of stubbornness and force of habit the Sami will carry on.

I said to Claes: 'Tell me about the migrations in the old days, when whole families moved.'

'You've got to go back to the 1950s, before that even. In Sweden, the wilderness that people love to talk about disappeared about a hundred years ago when communications improved and mining came to Kiruna and Gällivare. Samiland has been a recreation area since then.

The Sami who live between here and Karesuando were probably the last true nomads. They spent winters inland, north of Kiruna, and summers in Norway or near the border.'

'And the Sami from the Kiruna and Gällivare areas would have spent winters near those towns and summers in the mountains here.'

'Yes, or in Sarek. Many Sami have their winter homes in the forest, in or near Jokkmokk. During the summer they are in the Padjelanta National Park, where the mountains are low and grazing is good.'

'What would they have done month by month, season by season?'

'The nomad Sami have been called the eight seasons people. At the moment we're in late summer, what the Sami would call summer/autumn.'

'Each of our seasons is two seasons then?'

'Yes. There's spring/winter, spring, spring/summer, summer, summer/autumn, autumn, autumn/winter, winter, and then back to spring/winter. In spring/winter the herds are in the winterland, in the forest or near the coast. In spring they move to the calving places. The cows need peace and quiet; noisy tourists, for example, can upset the calving. When the calves are strong enough to walk – it doesn't take long – the herds move on to the mountains.'

'And in summer?'

'Summer is when the herds reach summer pasture. The main job there is marking the calves. Each family has its own mark which they cut into the calf's ear. In summer/autumn the reindeer are moved to the rutting ground. In autumn the animals are slaughtered. These days the meat is sold commercially.'

'And the antlers?'

'They're used for making souvenirs. It's difficult to live from herding alone so the Sami make souvenirs to bring in extra money. It's surprising what the tourists are willing to buy.'

'In autumn/winter then, the herds are moved back to winter pasture?'

'That's right.'

'Families don't travel by sled any more, do they?'

'Well, some people have to accompany the herds. These days it's usually done by a couple of adults on snowscooters, if there's enough snow. Families fly out later to join them or they drive. It means the women and children can spend more time in their houses in the winterland.'

'It'll be winter soon; autumn anyway. The birch leaves are changing colour. When will the snow come?'

'The first two weeks of September are usually good for walking. After that the weather changes quickly. The days get darker. Snow'll come in October, sometimes the end of September. You haven't got long left if you want to walk in warm weather. Where are you headed?'

'Riksgränsen, eventually.'

'Take you about a week to get there. Have you decided on a route?'

'Yes. I'll avoid the Kungsleden, go the other direction, east from here and on to Tarfala.'

'That's an easy walk. Won't take you more than a couple of hours. Tarfala's beautiful, lots of glaciers. There's a university research station there, people measuring how quickly the glaciers are melting. After Tarfala, where then? Vistas?'

'Yes, and Alesjaure – cross the Kungsleden there and walk to Unna Allakas.'

'Good choice. Not many places better than that. You can see Norway from there. During the war, when Norway was occupied, quite a few people escaped into Sweden at Unna Allakas. There was a mine there too. You can see the old buildings on the way to Riksgränsen.'

'They don't mine now?'

'No. The buildings have almost fallen down. A couple of houses, that's all.'

'It'll take about a week, you say.'

'You might be able to do it in five or six days. Go through it day by day. You'll be able to get halfway to Vistas on your first day; there's a wind shelter at Kaskasvagge where you can spend the night. Day two, you'll get halfway to Alesjaure. Easy walking, along the valley. Day three, you might as well camp at Alesjaure. Day four . . .'

'Unna Allakas. Just north of it there's a wind shelter. I'll stay there.'

'Okay. And day five'll take you to Riksgränsen. That's if you don't want any rest days and if the weather's good. Five days. It'll be tough. Are you fit?'

'Very.'

'And afterwards you'll be on your way to England?'

'I'm not going home yet. I'm going to carry on up to North Cape, take the Hurtigruten from Tromsø.'

'What do you want to go there for?'

'I've never seen it.'

'Nor have I. I wouldn't want to see North Cape.'

'Why not?'

'Tourists. Nothing but tourists: it's as far north as you can drive a car, that's why there are so many people. Stupid if you think about it. It's much better here.'

'I'd like to see the Norwegian coast.'

'Same thing. I know someone who did that trip, all the way from Bergen. You know what it was like? Awful. American tourists, that's all. I bet you most of them have never walked farther than to their cars.'

FOUR

Borderland

I have left Samiland and entered Scandinavia. The border is not fixed on a map, it is symbolic. The Sami represent contact with nature, they care for it, they understand it, worship it even.

Between Kebnekaise and Riksgränsen I saw a wolverine. It crossed my path as I was leaving a snow field. It ran, stopped, looked and ran, was in sight for thirty seconds only. But I will remember that animal for many years to come. Then came the ski resort Riksgränsen, Narvik and Tromsø. None left a mark on me. They don't belong to Samiland.

I saw my face at Riksgränsen, in a hotel mirror. It was bearded, tanned; the skin was tight: a reward for my walking. My chest, arms and legs had well-toned muscle, not a trace of fat. In the city I had suffered from headaches, colds, sore throats, allergies. In the mountains, not one day of sickness.

I recalled a sentence from a book, *The Sami Today and Tomorrow* by Tor Edvin Dahl: 'Everyone is convinced that it is more important to have a modern, advanced health service than work that forces the body to stay in peak condition.'

Idleness is a dangerous luxury.

In Narvik I was disturbed by people on the streets, the bright colours of their clothes, the ice cream and Coca

Cola that they tipped down their throats, the mopeds and motorcycles that screamed and rattled along the High Street.

I tried supermarket shopping for the first time in weeks, and was confused by the speed with which people chose and bought their goods. I stood at the dairy cabinet staring. Did I want bilberry yoghurt or raspberry, blackcurrant or strawberry? A woman pushed me aside without a thought or a word, grabbed two blocks of butter and threw them into her trolley.

At the youth hostel, I was close to shouting: teenagers everywhere, smoking, talking, drinking; feet on the tables, rucksacks in the corridors. The showers were filthy, clogged with hair and toilet paper. There were Inter-rail maps spread on the floor. Two days in Norway, two days in Sweden, forget Finland, back to Denmark and Germany, the sun, the south: this was travelling for the sake of it, to say that you had done it, the enthusiast's approach, tick it off in your guide book.

I didn't want to hear about Europe, or beaches, or the price of beer. When asked for an opinion or to share my food, I gruffly refused. A long-haired Swiss boy, staring at my block of Jarlsberg, asked: "Where are you from, man?' I told him to go away.

In the Swedish Seaman's Church, not far from the youth hostel, I met a Danish woman, Pernille, who was on her way home after a month in Finnmark, Norway's north-ernmost province. She spoke clearly and simply about the *vidda*, the mountain plateau where nomadic Sami live. She explained how Sami from Karasjok migrated during spring to Magerøya, North Cape's island.

I felt confident enough in her company to describe my Sarek walk, both the physical achievement and the psycho-logical battle that had taken place between Jimmy and me. We agreed in whispers that wild country can change a person, that it can speak to you.

Next day, we visited the war museum where I struggled to understand the events of April 1940 when the Germans and British fought for control of Narvik and the vital iron ore route from Kiruna. Only the ships' names stuck in my mind, *Gneisenau* and *Scharnhorst*. Pernille was irritated when I said that museums did not interest me. Outside we parted company. I went to the bus station, she went shopping.

Tromsø, with its 50,000 people, has been called the Paris of the North. If one likes night clubs – there are 19 – and restaurants, it is by far the liveliest town in Samiland. It is all of the things a modern town should be: a business centre, a conference centre, a home for musicians and writers and sports personalities. It attracts unemployed people from Troms and Finnmark counties and has Mack's, the world's northernmost brewery, 'the first beer on the North Pole'.

I dutifully visited the Polar Museum, the University museum and aquarium, and suffered the same symptoms I had in Narvik: drowsiness and a groaning stomach. At the campsite, my tent was pitched between two caravans: one German, one Norwegian. The Germans had a little fence with which they marked out their territory. Inside it were deckchairs, a collapsible table, a radio-cassette, and an inflatable dinghy. The Norwegians had a TV, which the woman of the family watched while she knitted. Both families were on their way home from North Cape.

Caravaning is an activity I find hard to understand or defend. Though your garden changes – mountains instead of a lawn – you are restricted to roads. The so-called beauty spots, where you are encouraged to park and spend the night, are usually filthy, ruined by families who would rather dump their rubbish under a bush than take it to the nearest bin or town.

Caravaners might think they are travelling in the wilds

but their presence proves the opposite. They harm Samiland, make it less impressive, less grand.

I think they should stay away.

FIVE

To Hammerfest and beyond

Every day, regardless of weather, the Hurtigruten steamers sail the coast of Norway between Bergen and Kirkenes. Fishing communities have grown to rely and depend on the ships for delivery of fresh food, post and other essentials. Even in winter storms, when planes are grounded, people know that the steamers will arrive and leave on time. As a money-earner, the ships transport tourists, about 20,000 each year, most of them wanting to see the midnight sun at North Cape.

In the autumn, when it's dark at night and tickets are cheaper, many of the cruise passengers are elderly people. At Tromsø, where I joined the Hurtigruten, my travelling companions were Americans, most of them over sixty, doing the Bergen-Kirkenes round trip. They were a lively bunch, and looked fit and well-fed. Most were dressed in bright velour leisure suits and thick-soled jogging shoes.

There were British passengers too, schoolteacher types in their forties. In contrast to the Americans, the men wore ties and leather shoes and the sort of blazers my father called sports jackets. The women wore dresses, unusual in northern Scandinavia, and cardigans in subdued colours. They were a disappointing sight and I was glad I would be with them for only two days, as far as Honningsvåg, 30km south of North Cape. Between Tromsø and there, the ship would call at Skjervøy, Hammerfest and Havøysund: two days, one night. I didn't buy a cabin ticket. The ticket woman said I could sleep in one of the lounges: 'All the young people do.'

Though the ship wasn't crowded, it was difficult to escape the other passengers. Wherever you sat you could hear their booming voices and energetic chit-chat. The Americans had guidebooks and maps on which they attempted to pinpoint the Hurtigruten's route. Some had trouble keeping track; others talked of North Cape as though it were a place of supreme importance. Its 300-metre cliff would be their reward for the days when nothing happened, when they doubted whether their thousands of dollars had been wisely spent. Card games filled the idle hours. Husbands, obviously unused to women's company, partnered their wives at whist. It was sad to see the strain on their faces, their shaking hands as tricks were lost, and to hear the quiet but cutting comments tossed across the table.

Away from the competitiveness of card games, when the Americans were on safe ground talking about family and home, their conversations could be touching. As we approached Skjervøy, two men recalled army basic training, how ludicrous it was, how ill-prepared they had been for war. Their talk drifted, sometimes stopped as one of them searched for a name or a suitable word. They spotted a trawler and wondered where it was heading, what type of fish it would catch. They looked out at Skjervøy's jagged, snow-clad peaks and agreed: 'Life must be tough up here.'

The English couples rarely raised their eyes from the *Guardian* or *Mail*. Perhaps, after four days and countless fjords, they had seen enough, run out of superlatives. Besides, there are few things the English love better than to read their newspapers abroad. How would they speak of Norway when they arrived home? Would they call it 'marvellous' and the scenery 'breathtaking'? Would they say that the weather might have been better, that it was

Skolt Sami woman from Sevettijärvi, Finland

Nomad Sami drawn by Aletta Ranttila, Finland

Nomad Sami drawn by Aletta Ranttila, Finland

Old reindeer watcher's cabin in the mountains near Kebnekaise

Mountain farm near Skibotn, Norway. Otertind in the background

Riksgränsen ski resort, Sweden

North Cape. Samiland's most popular tourist
attraction

Hurtigruten approaches Kirkenes

Skafferhullet, Kirkenes, on the Norwegian-Soviet border

Neiden Orthodox chapel, Norway

Wooden cross in graveyard at
Sevettijärvi, Finland: Ida Fofanoff,
born in Petsamo 1914, died in Ivalo
1988

Anna Björkman: farmer's daughter, nurse, skier

Cabins at Sevettijärvi. Reindeer skins nailed up to dry

so chilly some days they had to wear coats over their cardigans?

It had always bothered me that English tourists travelled so badly, that they could never merge with their surroundings. In Greece I could spot them from a distance by their clothes and their gait. My wife thought them funny and on the beach I was happy to laugh with her at their bloated bodies. In angry moments she went too far, calling me 'typically English; so smug, so arrogant'. That hurt.

Recently I had felt confident rather than arrogant. Though I had been in Sweden and Norway for only five weeks, my time in the mountains had washed away much of my city impatience, intolerance. I didn't fully understand the subtle changes and would have had trouble trying to explain them. How do you talk about mountains without sounding heroic, without over-emphasising physical achievement? How do you say that unspoilt land makes you feel at ease, or explain the calmness that comes when you stop expecting things to happen?

I had read many times about the Sami language, which has words with no equivalents in Norwegian, Swedish or Finnish, and enables them to express feelings a Nordic person would not understand or see to be important.

After my walk in Sareks and Kebnekaise I was a little closer to comprehending this. A Sami and a city person can look at the same mountain and see two different things. As a city person myself, I knew how they thought: a mountain is a leisure item, not part of working life. Mountains are for looking at or walking on. You can paint them, take pictures of them. If you see them in stormy weather, you might call them barren, desolate or inhospitable. If they are a long drive from the city, you call them remote. These are not words the Sami would use. When you live in the mountains, you are part of the landscape. The mountains are your home, your work place. The words you use, the thoughts you have, reflect your intimate contact with landscape and wildlife. Because city dwellers have lost this contact they do not know how to behave in the mountains. Their senses are dulled, their language lazy. Some of the words they use are not only inaccurate but hurtful and dangerous. Take 'wilderness' and 'wasteland', which imply an absence of civilised life. With these words you can deny the Sami's existence and their worth.

The Sami way of life – whether reindeer pastoralism, fishing or crofting – has never scarred nature, has left few visible traces of its existence, and this has made it easier for the state – the representatives of city living – to seize land. Governments and colonists said they could make better use of Samiland. They plundered its raw materials, harnessed its rivers for power. They opened mines and built towns. The remaining land, unproductive, was handed to the tourists, city dwellers with leisure time.

Sami who complained were called stupid, old-fashioned. Couldn't they understand that they would benefit from industry, that nomadism had no place in a modern economy? One can appreciate the Sami's scepticism. For them, development has meant destruction. In the name of education, they have been psychologically abused, constantly told that their language was not acceptable, was ugly. Their music, the *yoik*, has variously been condemned as the devil's work, as tuneless and boring.

These days pressure on them is less but still at work. Their culture is minority culture: the *yoik* is sung in the smallest halls; Sami literature reaches a tiny audience; Sami art is patronisingly called handicraft. It suffers from being useful – cannot be hung on walls but must be worn or held.

Even today's tolerance can have its side-effects. In fighting for Sami rights, they have had to learn political tricks, political language, the Nordic way of doing things. With every issue and election that is fought they become less Sami.

*   *   *

Excited chatter broke out when news reached the passenger lounge that we were approaching Hammerfest. Lenses with bayonet mounts were clicked into place, cameras were loaded, motor drives tested. An advance party of men with rucksacks and binoculars went on deck to reconnoitre. Women with handbags in their laps sat ready to go ashore.

'What's there to see?' asked one of them. 'What are we going to do?'

A friend told her: 'It's the northernmost town in the world. Seven thousand people live there.'

Did that mean there were shops, asked another woman.

'It's a town so there's got to be shops.'

One woman wanted to know if she'd be able to buy a Norwegian knitted jumper and was told that Norwegian knitted jumpers were cheaper in the States. A couple of the British contingent, who were listening to this, found it amusing. They smiled to each other, made knowing eyes.

With the town in sight, I joined the huddle of people waiting to go ashore. It was early morning, a clear, sunny day. The town looked bright, almost cheerful. Though we were as far north as the Yukon, Alaska and Greenland, it was warm enough to be central Europe.

Teenagers in the town square were eating ice cream and drinking Coca-Cola. A couple of German motorcyclists lounged on a bench eating breakfast. Three old men with walking sticks sat on a low wall, smoking. One of the tourists fired off a shot at that and at a dog tied to a post. I left the square and carried on up the hill, stopping at a supermarket and the fish factory. Here the town thinned out, so I crossed the road and doubled back, looking in the souvenir shops at what people were buying: sealskin pouches, leather purses with 'Hammerfest' stitched on, lurid car stickers and pictures of polar bears. Finding it all too jolly and junky, I returned to the ship to read.

*　　　*　　　*

The leg from Hammerfest to Honningsvåg takes nine hours, with a brief stop at Havøysund. After the exertions of Hammerfest, the passengers were quiet for the rest of the morning. Whist was played, guidebooks were read. Sunshine had given way to rain so the cameras and binoculars were put in their cases. Some passengers went to their cabins to sleep.

Shortly after Havøysund the captain announced that a whale had been sighted. The men grabbed their cameras and hurried away. The contingent left behind – those without cameras, binoculars and raincoats – asked what kind of whale it was, a big one or a small one. What was it doing? Was it swimming or jumping? Did whales jump? Did the others know, said a woman, that whales weren't fish?

'If they ain't fish,' said another, 'what are they?'

'Mammals,' said the woman. 'Mammals like us.'

'That figures,' said a third woman.

The men came back. 'We didn't see no whale. There weren't no whale to see. One of the guys on the bridge saw something he thought was a whale, that's how come they made the announcement. Me, I don't reckon there was a whale out there. We're too close to land for whales.'

'What do you know about whales?' asked his wife.

'I know that when a whale swims it don't do it close to land.'

'Maybe Norwegian whales are different,' said a woman.

'A whale's a whale,' said the man.

'No,' said another man, 'you've got different kinds of whales like you've got different ... cats and dogs.'

'Yeah, and they're still whales.'

'Did you get any pictures?' asked a woman.

'Of the whale we didn't see? That'd be a good picture.'

'I mean, did you get a picture of where the whale was supposed to be?'

'You want a picture of water, you can take my camera any time you like.'

An Englishman came into the lounge. He announced: 'I saw the whale.'

'You saw the whale,' said the Americans. 'Where?'

'At the back of the ship.'

'We've just been there and we didn't see it,' said a man with binoculars.

'I saw it just now. It was huge,' said the Englishman. 'It must have been after you left.'

'Are you sure it was a whale?' asked the man who knew about whales.

'Oh yes, it was a whale.'

'What did it look like?'

'It was big. It came out of the water and rolled over. Like this.' He showed us with his hand.

'A belly roll, huh? Did you get the shot?'

'Sorry?'

'Did you get a picture?'

'Unfortunately not. My wife has my camera and she's asleep.'

'It's always the same.'

'Afraid so.'

'Least you seen it,' said a woman. 'Which is more than I can say for these men.'

'Yes, I was very lucky,' said the Englishman.

SIX

A rock in the rain

A Norwegian man dressed in white and yellow strutted around the boat telling us we'd soon be arriving at Honningsvåg. He told the Americans to get ready to board the North Cape bus which would be waiting at the quayside; to put on raincoats and jumpers: 'It's going to be cold and wet.'

Jack, an Australian, was arguing with his wife. 'Christ, Jo,' he said. 'A bus trip to look at a rock in the rain. Can't see the point in that.'

'It's important,' said his wife.

'You go if you want to, love,' he said. 'I'm going to stay and read the paper.'

'I don't want to go alone, Jack.'

'Bloody hell, Jo. I don't have to follow you everywhere, do I?'

'I'll stay. It doesn't matter.'

'Go, Jo. There're plenty of others you can talk to.'

'No, no. I'll stay and knit.'

'All right, you win. Get your coat. We'll both go and look at the bloody rock.'

I waited until the boat had cleared before I left. It was raining hard. In front of me were a car park and a travel office, rain rushing down the glass in rivulets. I walked into the town and looked for somewhere to stay. I tried the hotel, got as far as the foyer and didn't like it. Back into the rain, past a shop selling English newspapers; headlines about the Royal Family. I tried the travel office, asked for a Hurtigruten timetable and the price of a ticket to Vadsø, further east. The woman didn't look at me as I spoke, slapped the leaflets on the counter in front of me, drew a red ring on the timetable at Vadsø.

Out on the tarmac, I thought of giving North Cape a miss, easier to get back on the boat, cruise another day to Vadsø or Kirkenes. Anything to get out of the rain, to have somewhere to sleep. I heard shouting from the direction of the boat, saw a man and woman coming down the gangplank; the man in front, bouncing down the steps, coat flapping in the wind. He stood on the tarmac, hands on hips, waiting for his wife. 'Where's the goddam bus?' he said and strode to the middle of the car park, towards me and a micro-van parked by the travel office. The woman caught up.

'Slow down, Henry,' she said. 'Don't get excited.'

'We missed the bus. I told you we'd miss it.'

'I'm sorry.'

'You had plenty of time to get your coat, Betty. But you had to go down at the last moment as usual. Now we've missed the goddam bus ... Hey, you!'

'What?' I said.

'Where's the bus?'

'I don't know. It's gone.'

'I can see that. Where'd it go?'

'To North Cape.'

'Does it stop on the way?'

'I don't know.'

'Did you see it?' asked Betty. 'Did you see where it went?'

'I didn't see a bus.'

'They could have waited,' said Henry. 'The gang knew we were coming. Why didn't they say anything? ... Where are you going, buddy?'

'To North Cape,' I said.

'How you getting there?'

'I don't know. I'm going tomorrow.'

'That's no good to us. We got to see it today, got to catch that bus. We'll get a car to take us.'

'We can't do that, Hen.'

'We paid for that trip. We're entitled to it. Where can we get a taxi around here?'

'I don't know,' I said. 'Ask in the travel office.' I picked up my pack to leave, to have another look in the town for somewhere to stay.

'Where're you going?' asked the driver of the micro-van who had been following our conversation.

'To find a place to sleep.'

'Are you going to North Cape?'

'Yes. Tomorrow.'

'Campsite's closed for the year. End of the season. The hotel's open.'

'I don't want the hotel.'

'There're some huts near Skarsvåg. They're open. It's pretty cheap.'

'Where's Skarsvåg?'

'Twenty kilometres from here. On the way to North Cape. Interested?'

'Yes.'

'You want a lift?'

'Sure.'

'It'll be a while yet. When my friend comes we can leave. He's doing some shopping.'

'Thanks,' I said.

'No problem. Get in the back.'

I settled down on some rags on the floor. The van stank of fish.

'Pain in the arse,' said the man.

'What is?'

'Americans.'

'Right, Americans.'

'Where do you come from?'

'England.'

'Your Norwegian is okay. England and Norway are good friends, you know. Always have been.'

'So people tell me.'

'It's true. Sea friends, you know what I mean?'

'Yes ... my name's David.'

'Yeah. Mine's Stein. Here's Ole.'

The back door banged open. A curly-haired man stood there, almost swung a sack on top of me. 'Who're you?' he said.

'David,' I said. 'Hello.'

Ole shut the doors, walked to the passenger seat. When he was inside, Stein said: 'David's coming with us to the camping. He missed the bus.'

'Nothing to see at North Cape this time of year,' said Ole. 'Look at the weather. Won't even be able to see the sea.'

'He's come this far,' said Stein. 'He might as well try.'

We drove through the town. I couldn't see anything. I was stretched out on the floor of the van, on the rags, in between a couple of sacks. Ole and Stein talked to each other about a woman who'd done something, or had something done to her. I couldn't make out what it was that happened ... The van made a noise like a hair dryer, whining on the flat, straining when it climbed a hill. Ole shouted over his shoulder: 'Are you going to look at Skarsvåg? You've got to see Skarsvåg.'

'Why's that?'

'It's the northernmost fishing village in the world. Have a look at it before you go to North Cape. Not a lot to see, of course: fishing boats, the factory, the church.'

I sat up as he spoke, looked past his bearded face to the windscreen wipers whirring. Outside, grey-green hills, no trees. Sea to our right. On we rattled.

'We'll be there in a minute,' said Stein. 'Couple of kilometres to go.'

I tightened my boot laces, pulled my cagoule from the rucksack pocket, pushed the pack closer to the door, and sat on it, waiting.

'Here we are,' shouted Ole. He jumped out, came to the back and opened the door. I laughed, seeing his hair stand on end in the wind. 'Hurry up,' he said.

I jumped on to the tarmac, pulled my rucksack on to one shoulder. 'Thanks,' I said and dashed for the huts. Rain was crashing on the tarmac, spitting up as it landed. I crossed a patch of grass, on to the car park, to a porch. I dropped the rucksack and hauled the door open.

A young woman with a towel wrapped round her head was standing inside, behind a chiller cabinet: three sad sandwiches on a plate.

'Hello there,' she said. 'Where did you come from?'

'Honningsvåg.'

'You need a room?'

'Yes. How much?'

'How long you staying?'

'One night.'

'In and out, right?'

'North Cape tomorrow.'

'You've come too late. Nothing to see now.'

'I'd like to get dry,' I said. 'Do you want me to pay now? Do you need my passport?'

'Just the money. One night, 100 kroner. Suit you?'

'Fine.'

'Okay. You get the hut nearest the toilet. Saves you running in the rain. Shower's round the corner.'

'Thanks.' I took the key and walked to the door.

'Hey! Money. I need the money.'

The cabin had two bunk beds, a heater, a little stove. It had dirty sheets, a dirty pillow. Between the mattress and the wall were dozens of black curly hairs. The wall looked like it had been used as a handkerchief. Graffiti by the headboard: 'Why does Tarzan live in Norway? ... 'cause he's king of the apes.' Dieter from Basle had slept there, two years ago; Svenja from Denmark, July 1986; Paulo from Milano, June 1987; Amanda from Stroud, no date. What the place needed was air. I unfastened the catches on the window, opened it a fraction, held the frame hard as the wind tried to rip it out of my hand. I stood fighting with the window for a while, then managed to slam it shut and attach the fasteners. I opened the door instead, sat in a chair and watched water streaming along the path outside.

I was hungry but didn't have any food worth eating: a can of mackerel somewhere, powdered potato, half a loaf of stale bread. I heard a car pull up outside, stood up to have a look; a Fiat with Spanish plates parked by a hut three down from mine. A man jumped out, a plastic bag over his head. He unlocked the door and called to the woman in the passenger seat. A skinny thing in high-heeled shoes, a newspaper over her head, dashed for the door. The man unloaded the car: he carried garden chairs, a hamper, suitcases – one black, one brown – and plastic carrier bags. He had a dustpan and brush in his hand when he called to me: 'Hello ... Terrible weather, huh?'

'Yes.'

'We're from Spain.'

'Nice to meet you.'

He ran for the door, came out a moment later and tipped the contents of the dustpan by the door. I went back to my chair and sat looking at the storm. I thought about boiling some water and making potato soup. Decided against it and went for a pee instead. More graffiti in the toilet: above the urinal: 'World's northernmost piss house'. Another: 'Jim. Glasgow. Cock of the North'. He wrote that in 1985.

Back in the hut, I thought some more about potato soup,

couldn't be bothered, thought about a shower, couldn't be bothered. I lay on the bed and read. Then I got up to look at the weather. If it hadn't been raining, I would have walked to Skarsvåg. I went back to bed, finished the book, started to read it again, didn't like it. I got my pot out, turned on the stove, sprinted to the toilet and filled the pot with a litre of water. I ran back to the hut and made potato soup; opened the door, sat and ate the soup and watched the storm.

It was still raining hard in the morning. I stayed in the hut as long as I could. At 11.30 the young woman came over and said she wanted me out by 12.00, otherwise I'd have to pay for another day. I set off with time to spare, held my thumb out for the first couple of cars that passed – a German, an Italian – but they didn't stop. After that I didn't thumb. I promised myself I'd walk all the way. If a car stopped, I'd say: 'No, thanks, I prefer to walk.'

Two hours later, I thought about hitching. In principle I was against it, and for a number of reasons. For a start, fifteen cars had passed including two British; not one of them looked as though it was willing to stop. The drivers had mean expressions. A couple of cars had splashed me, come so close I could have touched them. After that I walked in the middle of the road. Cars had to slow down and drive round. A couple tooted, Germans again. A Frenchman wound down his window and told me to eat shit. A minibus full of long-haired Italians stopped and asked what I was doing.

'Walking to North Cape,' I said.

'Where you walk from?' they asked.

'Athens.'

'You walked all the way from Athens?'

'All the way.'

'How long did it take?'

'Took me three weeks.'

'You walk fast, man. Good luck.'

A couple of motorcyclists stopped. They were English. 'Is this the road to North Cape?'

'Yes, it is.'

'You're English, too. We're from Sheffield. Yorkshire to North Cape. How about that?'

'It's a long way.'

'Norway's crap, isn't it? So expensive.'

'It's expensive, yes.'

'What are you doing?'

'Going for a walk.'

'Have you walked far?'

'From Stockholm.'

'You're joking?'

'No. All the way from Stockholm.'

'How long did it take?'

'Ninety-two days and a half.'

'Wow, that's something. Good luck to you, mate.'

An hour or so later, I saw a building and coaches and construction vehicles: North Cape. Soaked, but not tired, I walked to the door, left my rucksack on the ground and went in. Lots of shouting, lots of noise; people queuing to buy postcards and T-shirts. I gave that a miss, went to the cafeteria and bought two cheese rolls and a beer. At a table nearby, the English motorcyclists were getting ready to leave. One of them had a stack of postcards in his hand. They'd made it: Sheffield to North Cape by motorcycle. Now the home journey.

In front of me was a table of noisy Swedes, toasting each other with champagne. They were dressed in dark suits and ties and had blow-dried hair. Next to me an English couple were picking at their pastries.

'Awfully expensive here, isn't it?'

'Terribly. My cake's all right though. How's yours?'

'It's quite nice, actually. The coffee was a bit strong.'

'You should have put more cream in it.'

'I don't like cream in my coffee.'

'Really. I thought you did. They've got milk as well, you know.'

'No. I'm all right.'

I was still hungry. I bought a hot dog and a cake and another beer, took them outside and ate and drank while I walked. North Cape's cliff was behind the cafeteria building. I walked to a fence and a monument, looked over the fence and saw the sea, just. Still raining.

Lots of men lined up, taking pictures of their families. The Swedish men in suits came out and stood on the monument. One of them said they should take their trousers off. They asked a motorcyclist to hold the bundle. They asked the motorcyclist's friend to take the picture: four Swedes in their underpants a long way from home.

Two Englishmen walked to the fence. They looked at the sea.

'Here it is,' said one.

'Yes, North Cape,' said the other.

'It was named by an Englishman, you know. In the sixteenth century.'

'Yes. While we were looking for a north-east passage.'

'That's right.'

'Impressive, isn't it?'

'It is rather. Shame about the weather.'

'Yes. If only it hadn't been raining.'

'What's all that building behind us?'

'Some new development. They're improving North Cape, building a cinema, I think, and a sort of museum. It'll be ready next summer. They've got leaflets about it inside.'

The men stood and looked at the sea. Then one of them said: 'Seen enough?'

'Yes.'

'Better be getting back. The women will be wondering where we are.'

I left soon after, thinking I'd be able to get a lift back to Honningsvåg on one of the tourist buses. I tried the first one; no driver, but a woman near the front who asked in English what I wanted.

'To get to Honningsvåg,' I said.

'You're not with the group, are you?'

'No. Does that matter?'

'Our driver's awfully strict. You'd better ask him.'

'Can't I just get on?'

'It might cause a bit of trouble.'

I waited by the door. The driver approached. I asked in Norwegian: 'Can I buy a ticket to Honningsvåg?'

'No.'

'Are you going to Honningsvåg?'

'Yes, I am.'

'The lady said the bus is half full.'

'Nothing to do with it. The bus has been chartered and you're not with the group.'

'I'll pay.'

'No.'

'But if you're going to Honningsvåg, what's the problem?'

'I told you. You're not with the group and I'm not allowed to pick up hitch-hikers.'

Back to the building, pack on, walking again. At five kilometres an hour I could reach the huts in about two hours. Spend the night there and walk to Honningsvåg in the morning. Twenty kilometres: four hours. Forget about time and ships and going places. Walk. Look at the tundra.

An hour down the road, raining hard again, not looking at the cars as they passed but hearing them, the sounds of their engines a reminder of how slowly I was moving. Between cars, on the empty road, I settled into my own thoughts, pleased to pass a bend or a hill I had aimed for, trying to pick up the pace, aiming for six kilometres an hour.

Down a steep hill to my right, I saw a lake, a couple of people in a boat, rowing, nearly halfway across. I stopped and watched, trying to see whether they were fishing. Too far away. I moved on, a long descent followed by a climb to a bend in the road. I aimed for that. How long would it take? Ten minutes, try for eight. I was at the bottom going well, the rise in the road 30 metres in front of me. I heard a car behind, heard it coming, slowing, slowing to pass. I looked up. It was pulling in, 10 metres ahead, a Finnish car. The door opened, a man stuck his head out: 'Want a lift?'

The man opened the boot. 'Throw your pack in there. Come on, let's get out of the rain.' He introduced me to the passengers: two of them, his mother and father. Father was in the front passenger seat. I shook hands with the mother. She offered me a towel to wipe my face.

'Where are you going, friend? Honningsvåg?' asked the man.

'Yes. I'm going to catch the boat.'

'What time does it leave?'

'In an hour.'

'You'd never have walked it in an hour.'

'I was aiming for Skarsvåg today. Honningsvåg tomorrow. I'm trying to get to Karasjok.'

'We're going to Alta. You can drive part of the way with us if you like.' The man spoke to his parents. The mother put a hand on my knee. 'Okay,' she said.

I finished with the towel. The mother took it and put it in a plastic bag on the floor. She opened a small metal box and passed it to me. Sandwiches. I took one. She indicated I should take another. By the time we reached Honningsvåg I'd eaten five sandwiches, an apple, a handful of grapes and drunk a cup of coffee.

We caught the ferry to the mainland and drove quickly

southwards along the Porsanger fjord. They dropped me off at Russenes, where the road splits. The man's mother gave me a couple of sandwiches, an apple and a can of drink. I was standing by the road eating the apple when a group of Germans in a minibus stopped and asked whether I needed a lift. They were on their way to Sweden via Karasjok and Kautokeino.

SEVEN

Pure thoughts and deeds

A supermarket café in Karasjok, inner Finnmark. I have finished my coffee, pushed my cup across the table. No reason to leave yet. I'll sit a while. In front of me are three elderly people dressed in Sami clothes. Next to them is a table with teenagers. Their conversation switches between Norwegian and Sami. They are lively, noisy, like young children. One of them knocks over a glass and the others laugh.

The cashier has left her till and is sitting at a window table smoking a cigarette, raising her head when exhaling, blowing smoke high into the air. Outside, in the supermarket's car park, a couple of four-wheel-drive trucks – a Nissan and a Toyota – have pulled up and the drivers – two men, one in a baseball hat, one in a Sami cap – are chatting, leaning against the side of the Nissan. I can look at these men, or the people in the café, and see the themes that sum up Samiland: conflict between old and new; the loss of traditional values; Nordic dominance over the Sami.

I have facts and figures to back my argument. I can talk about alcoholism, violence and unemployment in the Sami heartland, the Finnmark *vidda*, the county towns of Karasjok and Kautokeino. I know that Kautokeino, for example, is the largest and most thinly populated county in Norway: 9867 sq km, 2962 people. You could tell a story using those figures alone.

The *vidda*, the mountain plateau at the top of Norway, is a perfect backdrop for tales of depression. Southern writers have described it as endless, dreary, windswept, isolated. Only birch and willow scrub, tundra pools and marshes. A sullen, unsmiling landscape. My feelings are different. I see strength in the *vidda*, resistance. I see pride in the small, shabby towns. I have become dismissive about dates and numbers and percentages. They confuse me, bore me. Instead, I look at gestures, at faces as people speak. I seek out quiet places and quiet people, and look and listen.

Music of the *vidda*. The *yoik*: rhythmic, hypnotic, repetitive, rising and falling in easy curves like the landscape, like the people, the animals, the seasons; trickling and tumbling like water. Yoiking: 'The art of remembering other people'.

Art of the *vidda*. My knife. Of all I own, my knife is the most important to me, the most useful. I have cut wood with it, gutted fish, sliced bread, opened bottles and tins, cleaned my nails, scraped mud from my boots. It hasn't left my side since Kvikkjokk. I have grown to like its bounce as I walk or run, its weight on my left hip, always there, always ready to be used. It fits my hand. It sits in my hand. Sami art: pleasing to look at, a pleasure to use. My knife is the difference between past life and now. It isn't a weapon, isn't offensive. That I eat with it and clean my nails with it are proof that I have taken sides, that I don't want the city. Besides, a nail file would be too much trouble; I would lose it.

I don't need to own many things. In this Karasjok café, I don't need polished shoes, a suit and tie, a stylish hair cut, a way with words, a car, a wallet full of money. Even my camera spends more time packed than unpacked. That reflex action – reach for the camera – has been forgotten. These days I look first, at light as it changes, at animals and birds, their movements and colours, their noises. Instead of using my camera, I think: *Remember this moment.*

*   *   *

The Sami are at one with their surroundings. To me, that is their strength. I have simple views of Samiland: Understand the Sami and you can have pure thoughts of nature, your actions can be clean.

In Samiland there is everyday work of which I am not a part. It is proof of the Sami's resilience: the Sami Institute in Kautokeino, the Sami high school in Karasjok, the Sami parliament of Finland, and preparations for parliaments in Sweden and Norway. Sami radio at Karasjok, Kiruna and Inari. Sami newspapers: *Samefolket*, *Nuortanaste*, *Sagat*, *Sami Aigi*. Sami writers past and present: Matti Aikio, Hans Peder Jalvi, Anders Larsen, Johan Turi, Hans Aslak Guttorm, Eino Guttorm, Pekkabuk Kari, Kirsti Palto, Nils Aslak Valkeapää, Sylvia Blind, Andreas Labba, Sara Ranta Ronnlund, Paulus Utsi, Nils Victor Aslaksen, Magne Einefjord, Inger Haldis Halvari, Ailo Gaup, John Gustavsen, Magnar Mikkelsen. Sami artists past and present: Nils Nilson, John Andreas Savio, Lars Pirak, Ilmari Tapiola, Johan Rist, Iver Jåks. These people define Samiland, give it strength, give it shape.

Behind me are miles and months. I have not spoken for five days. When I think, it is in a mixture of Scandinavian and English, thoughts which drift. For the past week there has been me and the forest, the Finnish forest near Lake Inari. Late summer is turning into autumn. The birch trees are golden, the bilberry bushes heavy with fruit. The nights are colder. Leaves and light rain, falling every day.

I have been thinking about the distant past when reindeer were wild and the Samis' forefathers caught them in pits which they dug in the forest. In those days, before the sixteenth century, only small herds of domesticated reindeer were kept. They were used as draught animals or decoys when hunting.

A group of families, known as a siida, used common hunting and grazing grounds. Traps, snares and pits were owned collectively. There were strict rules on how resources were to be divided, with priority given to hunters.

The Sami trapped fur-coated animals: beaver, bear, squirrels and wolves. Big rivers became important trade routes. This lasted until the seventeenth century when the fur trade declined. The wild reindeer population decreased dramatically owing to over-hunting. By the beginning of the twentieth century, wild reindeer were extinct in Finland. The last beaver was shot in 1861.

Today, wolves and bear remain, though only Finland of the Nordic countries has more than a handful of wolves. Many drift in from the Soviet Union. The wolf is a hated animal. It attacks sheep and reindeer. When there's a wolf in the forest, parents lock up their children as though a rapist is on the prowl. Bears, wolverine and lynx can do as much damage, but who would argue that they should be wiped out? Wolves are run down by snowscooters, their heads smashed by axes.

From wolves to women. What did Sami women do? Looked after their men most of all. In nomad households, women were the first to get up in the morning. They made the fire, made coffee, fed their husbands. They collected and chopped wood, fetched water, milked the reindeer. During migrations women made meals using wind-dried meat and bread. They looked after the children, they fished and collected senna grass, which was used to line their family's reindeer-skin boots. Women made clothes: jackets, trousers, belts, shoes, mittens and caps. They made dog food, using reindeer blood boiled with flour, water and salt.

Travelling is not the best way of taking in the details. With a cabin in the woods or in the mountains, I would learn so much more. A base, a place to live, so that I could wander the same paths day after day, see the same mountain under summer light and winter snow. I am ready to settle here. I wish Samiland were my home. Forest thoughts, I know. A town, people, roads, cars would set me racing again. Moods can change from day to day, minute to minute. Sunshine warms me, cheers me; black clouds can make me doubt that I belong.

I would like to be with one person, one woman.

I have nothing to offer and everything to gain. I thought learning was remembering, and that understanding came when you remembered enough. By my fire, by its light, I know there are different ways of thinking.

Samiland has suffered from foreign thoughts and deeds – Chernobyl, Alta, acid rain, overfishing, industry that scars, the taking of land. These were not accidents, but actions which came from destructive thoughts, our incorrect way of looking at nature.

Circumstances may demand that I return to that world, but if given a choice I would live in Samiland.

Lifts took me to the border at Näätämö. I travelled from there along the rocky Varanger fjord to Kirkenes, a Norwegian mining town near the Soviet border. I stayed there for a day at the sort of guesthouse where men sleep in their socks and drink vodka in the morning.

Not one Norwegian town has said welcome, not one has asked me to stay. So I planned the next step, a journey to Murmansk. I handed over my passport, applied for a visa. Our group will leave in three weeks. I will travel to the forest to wait, to Pasvik, the finger of Norwegian land between Finland and the Soviet Union.

EIGHT

Living with the night

Pasvik National Park: Day One

My home for the next two weeks is the log cabin called
Ellenkoia. I have brought no food with me, will have to
catch it or gather it. Five kilometres west is Finland, to the
east is the Soviet Union. Not far from here, border guards
are patrolling with guns and dogs; Soviet soldiers are sitting
in their watchtowers.

I can hear nothing, not even the wind. Outside are
birch and pine trees, the birch glowing gold, leaves falling
whether there's wind or not. In the grass between trees
are dwarf cornel and bilberry, bog whortleberry and cranberry. In the shade of rotting stumps grow huge boletus
mushrooms.

The cabin is big enough to sleep six, with reindeer skins
on its low bunk beds, a stove, a mop and bucket, a table
and two stools and a fishing net. Hanging outside the door
are two axes and a set of reindeer antlers. On the ground
are perch and pike skins, and in a birch tree near the
lakeside are two pike skeletons with flesh on the heads.

In the two hours before nightfall I picked a litre of bog
whortleberries and half a pot of mushrooms. I made a
mousetrap using the bucket, two sticks and some breadcrumbs which I found under the table. If it works, I will
set more and make soup with the meat. I placed the bucket
in a dip in the ground on a well-used mouse run, one stick
up the side of the bucket and the other over the rim,

trimming it until it fitted the rim's width exactly. Any pressure and it would fall in the bucket. On the sticks I sprinkled a few pinches of breadcrumbs and left the bucket until morning.

With the sun almost down over the pine trees around Ellenvatnet I fished for perch, casting out as far as I could, using a bright 10gm lure and two BB shot for extra weight. I stood for an hour but caught nothing. I must find a better way of fishing. Perhaps the net is the answer. Shame there's no rowing boat.

Nights are going to be long. After 8pm, it's too dark to work so I'll have to lie in my sleeping bag until I fall asleep. Normally I sleep at midnight or after. I hope as I get hungrier I'll get tireder and will be able to sleep early: 8pm till 6am would be good enough.

I am writing this by the light of the stove. For reasons I don't yet understand, I feel less secure in this cabin than I would in my tent. At the moment I am not worried but – and I don't like to write this – I am afraid to look out of the window. The darkest place is next to a dim light.

Day Two
Success, the mousetrap works. Alive in the bottom of the bucket was a tiny brown mouse. I didn't know how to kill it and didn't want it to bite me so I poured water in the bucket and drowned the animal. I skinned it carefully with my Helle knife, not wanting to burst the intestines. I pulled the skin off over its head, boiled the carcass with a couple of mushrooms. Tasteless. I should have brought some salt. Tonight I'll set three traps.

I spent the rest of the morning picking two litres of bilberries and bog whortleberries, only the big, sweet berries. I'll eat some fresh and boil the rest. I didn't need so many but enjoyed working. Keep busy, keep thinking.

I have stopped collecting water from outside the hut and walk instead to a stream ten minutes away. I think the water from there tastes better. It should be a good fishing spot too. If I caught a small fish, a perch or a grayling, I could dead-bait for pike. A 3kg pike would give food enough for three days, maybe longer.

I want to make some snares but there's no wire in the hut. I might try using fishing line. The problem would be getting the line to grip the animal's neck. Think it over. A bootlace might be better. I could line it with fish hooks so that they dug into the hare's neck as it struggled. So far I'm not hungry enough to pursue the idea further. I am tireder today, so sleep shouldn't be a problem.

Day Three

I don't feel like writing today. I have nothing to write about. I am angry. None of the mousetraps worked and I haven't caught any fish. Berries and mushrooms, that's all there is to eat.

Day Four

I walked to the national park boundary looking for somewhere to fish. One place looked likely, where a stream flowed into a pond. Lots of weeds and more than a metre deep. I fished for an hour and a half, caught nothing but there were a couple of bites. Why didn't I catch them? Perhaps they were too small. Not to worry.

I feel good today. On the way back from the fishing trip, I sat by the shore of Ellenvatnet leaning against a birch tree. A reindeer ambled through the trees to the water, can't have been more than 30 metres away. He nosed around, stepped in and swam to the other side, nearly 100 metres. I hope to see elk.

The walk tired me out and I went to bed at 6pm.

Day Five

I am hungry, not so much for quantities of food but for tastes. I miss salt and sugar. The food I'm eating is either acidic or tasteless. I've got the shits. Need to crap every hour, sometimes less.

Today I'll give the berries a miss and concentrate on fishing. I'll walk south and collect mushrooms on the way, look out for hare runs and burrows. I've been thinking I might be able to catch birds by putting a baited hook on the ground. Tie the hook to some fishing line. No reason why it shouldn't work. But I've got no bait. Which birds eat berries? I'd like to catch one the size of a crow or a seagull.

Have learnt a useful lesson. Finding food takes the entire day. Time has to be used productively. Picking berries takes little time and wastes little energy. Hunting with a bow and arrow would demand a lot of energy and there's no guarantee of success. I wish it weren't true: I need meat.

It's 5pm. I'm back from the fishing trip. I need to record this in detail, to understand my feelings. First, I caught a fish, a grayling. I had been spinning for an hour, was on my last five casts. I felt miserable. My days in Pasvik seemed pointless. I was thinking of walking to the bus stop at Vaggatem and getting off at the first food shop. I knew what I would buy: goat's cheese, rye bread, milk and bananas, and a beer to celebrate. But the bite stopped all that. The lure was no more than five metres out. I was retrieving slowly. The line thumped and I struck. The fish fought hard for a short time and suddenly gave up. I pulled it to the surface. It rolled on its side. On the bank, it hardly struggled, was dead after one knock with the handle of my sheath knife. I gutted it straight away; its heart was still pumping, opening and closing like a tiny fist. Along its sides were thin strips of roe which I scooped out with my fingers and ate raw. I slit open its swollen stomach to see what it had been eating: dozens of snails packed tight.

I grilled it over the embers of a pine fire. After only fifteen minutes the meat peeled off the backbone in juicy, white lumps. Perfect. It didn't need salt or butter or herbs. I know that if I don't eat for another three days I'll be all right. And there's no need to put the mousetraps out for a while. Tomorrow I'll go fishing again.

Day Six

Nights are worrying me. I have started to listen to the night. Animals walk around the hut. I know they do. I see the tracks in the morning. Last night it was a reindeer. My reaction was understandable but stupid. I heard movement, heard snorting and reached for my knife. I sat in bed waiting for the door to open, for someone to come in. Later, when the animal had gone, I could sleep only with my back to the log wall and my knife near my pillow.

This morning I took the two axes from above the door and hung them inside the hut. Why? I didn't want someone to steal them and use them against me at night. A silly thing to think, I know. There's no one here who'll harm me.

The sun was stronger this morning so I had a dip in the lake. I dived in and shot back out again, dancing on the bank, my feet and shins in pain from the cold. Instead of taking pictures, as I usually do when the light is good, I sat and watched how the birch leaves shimmered, so cleanly outlined, so crisp against the background of a deep blue sky.

I went fishing and caught nothing. Dreading the night time.

Day Seven

Halfway there. In a week I'll be at Storskog, waiting to cross the border into the Soviet Union. I've been giving some thought to the type of people I'll be travelling with: probably old communists, mostly men. They'll talk about the war, tell me about the liberation when Soviet troops crossed the border and chased out the Germans. 'The Russians are our friends' – that'll be the message of my Murmansk companions.

I know that my days in the forest are valuable. In the future I will remember the smells, the colours, the silence. But there are moments when the trees seem to smother me, when I long for open country. Murmansk will be ugly, noisy, not part of Samiland. But perhaps I need that for a while, people to speak to. I want meat and fresh vegetables. I want strong coffee and vodka. I want the company of young women.

I think I've got an infected bladder. There isn't a moment when I don't feel like peeing, a constant pressing below my stomach. When I try to pee, there're a few drops at most. Which makes me think that lots of vodka will sort it out. Disinfect my system. But now, should I drink a lot of water or should I not drink at all? I'm worried. I don't want to visit a doctor; I have no medical insurance. I won't eat any more mice and I'll wash all berries before eating them. I won't eat any more raw roe.

I went fishing and caught nothing. I'm seriously hungry. My stomach feels tight. I think the pain from my bladder is spreading down. I don't want to think about it.

Day Eight
I'm too ill to write. I want to leave. I'm lying in bed looking at my photographs of Aris and Alexandra. I miss them. If I could fly to Greece now, I would. Night time is coming. I hope I can sleep.

Day Nine
I'm ill but I know I have to eat. I have to catch a fish. I have to move, think ahead. How about this? Soon I'll be on my way to the Soviet Union. Food, more food than I'll be able to eat. I could leave today and spend three days in

Kirkenes. It wouldn't be giving up. I've been here more than a week, without food, without company, without seeing anyone. I haven't any clean clothes and I need clean clothes for the Murmansk trip. I need at least two days to look around the shops, to rest, to get well again. Why not leave tomorrow morning? I'll stop writing now and think about it.

4.30pm. I'm staying. Of course I can't give up. Why not? I caught a small grayling and I'm going to night-line it for a pike. Here's the plan. I'll thread hooks through its body, make a trace with six strands of 5lb line. I don't think a pike will be able to bite through that. I'll leave the reel's bale arm open and secure the rod to a tree.

Day Ten

I'm going to check my rod now. I'm hopeful there's a fish on the line. I've been assuming it'll be a pike but it could be a perch. No matter. Both are good food fish.

An hour later. I knew it, I knew it; I willed that fish on to the line. The moment I picked up the rod I knew I'd done it. Here's how it happened ... I flicked the bale arm closed and reeled in the slack, lots of it. Then I felt the resistance, a dead weight, but I knew it wasn't the bottom because the weight kept coming, like reeling in a boot. About 20 metres out the fish started to fight. I didn't want that. I didn't want the fish to bite through the line. I let him go, let him run. I sat on a rock and was willing to stay there all afternoon.

I reeled in again, this time forcing him, feeling he wanted to run but not letting him. He was tired: a fresh fish fights hard, doesn't stop; this one was finished. I got him in close, pulled his head to the surface. I saw I'd hooked both jaws. He couldn't open his mouth. That meant I could force him in, beach him. From what I saw of his head, I reckoned he weighed 6lbs, food for the rest of my time in Pasvik.

I pulled him up to the bank, reached with my right hand

into the water, only a few inches from the fish's snout and hauled, a clean movement up and out of the water, tossing him on to the bank. He thrashed and whipped. For a moment I didn't know what to do; I thought of hitting his head but he wouldn't stay still. I didn't want to touch him, not with those teeth and hooks in his mouth. So I stabbed him in the head and twisted, watched the dark, creamy blood bubbling from the wound and felt the fish dying. The tail-whipping got weaker and weaker until the only movement I could see was a twitching around the gills. I pulled the knife out and wiped it on my trousers, walked elated to the cabin where I gutted and filleted the fish.

I made a fire with pine logs and grilled one of the fillets, hanging the remaining meat from a tree. No flies at this time of year. On a corner of the fire I stewed a small amount of bilberries and used it as a sauce over the meat. Afterwards I drank a litre of cold water and went to bed.

Day Eleven

Nights are better now. The noises do not bother me. To prove the point I have moved the axes to their proper place above the door outside. I swept the hut and washed the floor with warm water. Getting ready to leave. My stomach has settled but I still have the bladder problem, am learning to cope with the discomfort and pee when I need to.

I am smug today. I've been thinking that few people would willingly spend eleven days in the forest without food. Not if they knew there was a bus stop one day's walk away. If I left now I wouldn't be cheating. I know that I could carry on catching food.

What would friends say if I told them about my fortnight here? What would be their first question? I think they'd ask why? And I would say: 'I needed to find out whether I could live here and like it.'

I have succeeded. The months in Samiland have helped me. If my first weeks had been spent here alone, instead of in Sarek with Jimmy, I would not have coped. I would have been frightened, by the noises at night and the absence of noise during the day; and by time, which some days refused to pass.

NINE

Long weekend in Murmansk

I

There were thirteen of us waiting to cross the border at Storskog. It was dark. The only lights I could see came from the Norwegian border cabin behind us. In front was a yellow and black barrier and 10 metres beyond that the Soviet Union. We couldn't cross immediately, said the Norwegian officer who had walked with us from the cabin. We had to wait for one of the Russian border guards to give the signal: our invitation to step into the Soviet Union.

I hadn't spoken to the people I was travelling with but by listening as we waited I got an idea where they came from. Some metres behind me was a party of Swedes, who seemed to know each other well. There were seven of them; six were women. To my left stood a tall Norwegian man in his early thirties; he had his arm around a woman, also tall, with spiky brown hair. She carried a knapsack; the man had an aluminium briefcase and a leather holdall. On my right was a thin elderly man. I hadn't heard him speak to anyone but I could see from the passport he held that he was Norwegian. In his right hand he had a Russian phrase book.

Next to him stood two women. One was in her sixties, the other couldn't have been much more than nineteen. The older woman was saying she didn't like waiting in the cold, that ritual and formality were a lot of nonsense; why couldn't we simply walk under the barrier and get on the bus which was waiting for us? She was American or

Canadian. The woman with her was dressed like a Greek fisherman: cap, a canvas jacket and baggy black trousers which were short of her ankles. She wore black suede shoes without socks and had a duffle-bag over her shoulder. She was English.

'I don't mind waiting. I think it's rather exciting,' she said.

'We're just a bunch of tourists,' said the other woman. 'Why are they treating us like spies? I can see that Russian soldier sitting in his hut over there. He's not doing anything. He could let us in.'

The Swedes were laughing. One of the women said: 'You're disgusting, Christian.'

The man said: 'That's not all. I was alone in physio-therapy and these gorgeous women came in with a tape recorder. They plugged it in and did stretching exercises to disco music. It was like Jane Fonda. From where I was lying I could see right up their legs. I put twenty kilos more on the bar.'

'To impress them,' said one of the women.

'Right. I grabbed hold of the bar and strained to lift. What happened? I let out a bloody big fart.'

'God, no,' said one of the women. 'You didn't. What did they say?'

'Told me to blow my trumpet somewhere else.'

A Russian soldier in high boots and green uniform approached his barrier, tugging at his cuffs as he walked. At the barrier he nodded to his Norwegian counterpart and we lifted our bags, ready to walk. After an exchange of words, the Russian asked us to step forward. He led us to a dimly-lit hut. Here, he said, we had to fill in a customs declaration, saying how much money we had and listing all photographic, electrical and computer equipment.

'Do you mean everything?' asked the Norwegian with the aluminium case.

'Everything,' said the soldier.

'It'll take a long time,' said the man.

'It doesn't matter,' said the soldier.

I was the first to finish my form. I listed: One Canon A1 camera. One FD 28 mm lens. One FD 85 mm lens. Ten rolls of colour slide film... Currency: 1000 Norwegian kroner, £100 in travellers' cheques.

The soldier, now standing behind a counter, said, 'You are British? Not Norwegian?'

I said: 'Yes, I am British.'

'You like photography?'

'I do.'

'You will take many pictures in Murmansk?'

'Yes, I will.'

'You have any guns or ammunition or drugs?'

'No.'

'You have any books, magazines or other reading matter?'

'Yes.'

'Let me see, please.'

I gave him my two books. He put one on the counter and looked at the cover of the other. He flicked through the pages. 'What are these about?'

'Action. Adventure.'

'You like these kinds of books?'

'Yes.'

'They are English?'

'No. American. Elmore Leonard is American.'

He put the books on the counter and pushed them towards me. He said: 'You can go now. Have a good time in Murmansk.' He pointed to the exit.

Outside stood a short, stocky man with a beard. He had black curly hair and wire-framed glasses. He wore a blue anorak, jeans and white training shoes. He said: 'Your name, please?'

'David.'

'Hello, David.' He held out his hand. We shook.

'Welcome to the Soviet Union. My name is Sergei. I am your guide and translator. Please wait in the bus for the others.'

I chose a seat near the front, five rows back. The young English woman was second person on. She said her name was Katherine, asked me not to call her Kate.

'And I'm David,' I said. 'Not Dave.' She asked whether she could sit next to me, so that I could translate for her. She told me she was a music graduate looking for work in Norway as a church organist.

'There's a lot of call for organists,' she said. 'I'm thinking of working in Fauske.'

The best I could do was: 'Have you played the organ long?'

'Ten years,' she said. 'I play the clarinet too. But I'm no good at that.' I told her that I didn't play any instruments but I wished I could, the drums preferably. Katherine said she didn't like drums.

Third on was the elderly woman. 'I've met Kate,' she said. 'But I don't know you. My name's Billy. Funny, I know, but that's what I'm called. To save you from asking, I'm from Canada. I've lived in Vardø for twenty-six years.'

When everyone was on the bus, Billy stood up: 'You probably want to make a speech, Sergei. Before you do, I think we ought to introduce ourselves. I hate not knowing who I'm travelling with. My name's Billy. What are your names?'

'Arne.' The elderly man.

'Hugo.' The tall Norwegian.

'Ellen.' His friend.

'David.'

'Katherine.'

The Swedes: 'Mai-Lis' ... 'Mia' ... 'Katarina' ... 'Christian' ... 'Eva' . ... 'Mariana' ... 'Anna'.

'Okay,' Billy said. 'You can make your speech now, Sergei.'

'Thank you,' said Sergei. 'To begin with, language problems. We have many nationalities with us today. I will speak Norwegian – Sergei Norwegian. It's not the best in the world and I apologise for that. If any of you have trouble understanding me, say so and I'll try again.'

'Can you speak up?' said Christian.

'Yes, and you can move forward. You don't need to sit at the back. Now then, we will drive in this bus to Nikel. Many of you will have heard of the town. I know that you can see it from across the border. All I want to say now is that Nikel is an important mining town where 20,000 people live. Ten thousand of them work in the mine. We won't stay in Nikel. We'll catch a train from there to Murmansk. The trip to Nikel will take about half an hour, maybe more, definitely not less. The train journey will take eight hours. Any questions?'

'Yes,' said one of the Swedes.

'Name, please.'

'Mia. Will we have to sit up all night on the train?'

'No. The train is a sleeper. Four people to each compartment. We will arrive in Murmansk early in the morning and will proceed directly to the hotel. The hotel, called Arctica, is a minute by bus from the station. When we arrive, we will book in and eat breakfast. The Arctica is a first-class hotel. It has two restaurants: one with buffet service, where you will eat during the day and most evenings, and one with waitress service for parties. Do you like parties? . . . Good. There will be music too, played by a band. More of that later. In the hotel there is also a *bureau de change*, an Intourist office, and an international telephone exchange. You will sleep two people to a room. There is a bath and toilet with each room. Any questions?'

'Yes . . . I'm Christian. Is there a bar in the hotel?'

'Of course. There are two bars. One for drinks only, and one in the restaurant with table service. You can buy beer, Russian or Western, champagne and vodka, plus the usual things you find in any bar. Okay?...Now I want to tell you about Murmansk. It is a young town, founded in 1916 to take advantage of ice-free waters in the Kola fjord. Just like the coast of Norway, it benefits from the Gulf Stream. It is the world's biggest town north of the Arctic Circle: 450,000 people live there and by the end of the century it will house half a million. It was nearly destroyed by the Germans in the Second World War but was never occupied. Today it is a modern industrial town with theatres, cinemas, schools, research institutes and the district of Murmansk museum. The main industry is fishing and you will have the chance, if you wish, to visit a factory ship. Murmansk is also the home port of the atomic ice-breakers – *Lenin*, *Arctica* and *Sibir* – and it is the starting point of the north-east passage. Any questions?'

'Yes.'

'Your name, please.'

'Arne. You said that we could look at a factory ship. I don't know about the others but I'd like to do that very much. Are there any other arranged visits?'

'Of course. You will be able to visit a polyclinic for building workers, a Pioneer leisure centre, monuments and statues, a sports stadium and Murmansk museum.'

'I have a question. My name is Anna. There are seven of us from Sweden, all nurses in Kirkenes. We were told by the travel office that there would be visits related to our job. We don't mind visiting factories and ships but we would prefer hospitals. Is that possible?'

'Correct me if I am wrong, but I don't think you are all nurses,' said Sergei. 'What we have done is arrange a varied programme. The polyclinic will be of interest to you. There you will see modern and traditional methods of treatment. At such short notice I do not think that other visits related to your work can be arranged.'

'Sergei,' said Mia, 'if for some reason we don't want to visit ships and factories, can we stay in the hotel or walk around town? I read that there is a Berjoska in Murmansk.'

'You are free to do as you choose. Yes, there is a Berjoska in town. For those of you who do not know, Berjoska is a shop where you pay in Western currency. They sell souvenirs and drink. Any more questions? ... No. Good. Let's go to Nikel.'

As the bus moved off I sat with my hands cupped around my face looking out of the window.

'What can you see?' asked Katherine.

'Trees,' I said. 'Trees and bushes.'

'Nothing else?'

'It's too dark. There're trees by the side of the road, that's all.'

Katherine asked questions about the train journey to Murmansk. I hadn't translated as thoroughly as she would have liked. She wanted to know exactly where the cinemas were located and what was playing at the theatre. What kind of monuments would we visit? What did I mean by a factory ship. What did they do on a factory ship? I explained that they froze fish.

'I don't want to look at frozen fish,' she said.

'It's not compulsory.'

After five minutes or so, the bus stopped at a wire barrier across the road. I peered out and saw a spotlit fence which stretched across country into the distance. Katherine wanted to know what it was. 'It's a fence.'

'I thought we'd crossed the border.'

'This one's to stop them getting out,' I said.

Sergei waited on the road by the front of the bus. Beyond him, by the barrier, was a small cabin with a dim light inside. Sergei walked to the barrier and looked through. A couple of soldiers ambled into view. One had a torch strapped to his shoulder. They exchanged a few words with Sergei and went into the hut. There was a clicking at the gate: an electric lock. The soldier with the torch waved us through.

Billy shouted: 'Hey Sergei, what was that?'

'A checkpoint.'

We drove on through birch wood. I looked out at the night. Katherine moved next to Billy and they struck up a conversation with Arne. He didn't speak English, so Billy translated. Hugo was up front talking to Sergei. Ellen seemed to be sleeping. The Swedes were telling each other stories, talking about doctors and patients at the hospital.

Ten minutes later we stopped at another barrier. Again it ran across country, through woods and over bog. Sergei got off and looked into the window of the hut. Back on the bus he said: 'I'm sorry, this may take some time. All we can do is wait.

Cold air blew in through the open door, so cold that I crossed my arms and put my hands under my armpits. I lifted my feet and pressed my knees against the seat in front. We waited.

Sergei was saying to Hugo: 'I don't know, I really don't know how long it's going to take ... not usually this long, no ... there should be someone here soon ...'

Christian said: 'Nikel's such a popular place they need fences to keep you out.'

Billy turned and said to him: 'Have you ever seen Nikel? It spews out more than 200,000 tonnes of sulphur a year. It's poisoning Finnmark, day and night, non-stop.'

'Two hundred thousand tonnes,' said Christian. 'What's that every hour?'

'A hell of a lot,' said Billy.

Sergei got back on the bus. 'I think someone is coming now. It won't take long.'

A young soldier was walking towards the bus, swinging a light so the beam caught the ground and wire of the fence. He was wearing a huge peaked cap, an ill-fitting coat and high leather boots. He climbed the steps, looked in through the door, nodded a greeting to the driver and shone his light at our faces. First at Billy, then Katherine and Arne, at Ellen sleeping, at me and back at the Swedes. He looked at Hugo who was sitting on the front seat. He stepped into the bus and walked along the aisle shining the light on empty seats. He looked at the luggage racks and bent down to look under the seats. He walked to the end of the bus and shone the light into Christian's eyes. The soldier didn't speak. He looked at the bags the Swedes had with them, shone his light at Mia and Mai-Lis, turned and walked slowly to the front. He stopped by me, looked, shone the light in my face, stared as I shielded my eyes, and then walked to the door.

We drove on along the shore of a lake. I could make out faint lights on its far side and, closer to the road, timber cabins and what I thought were boats. Running alongside the road was a high wire fence. All trees between the road and the fence had been uprooted. Some had been cleared, others lay there in bundles on the wet earth and rocks.

'There's Nikel,' shouted Arne. I turned and saw huge smokestacks above a jumble of buildings. Over them was a halo of bright blue light; beyond it, the black night sky. From the stacks rose thick plumes of smoke, arced by the wind. Closer now: we were heading towards the Nikel works. A mess of tumbledown wooden huts and fences and sheets of metal; kilometres of metal piping, winding round and round the buildings, steam escaping from thick black pipes. Closer: hearing thumping, banging, hissing. Looking down on to the plant and seeing bare, black ground; spotlights shining up at the smokestacks.

Past the plant, down a hill with a footpath alongside. Earth bulldozed and piled high. No trees or plants. Lumps of twisted metal and piping lying in heaps by the roadside. Down the hill: a man pushing a pram. He was wearing a fur hat, the ear-flaps down, tied under his chin. As the bus passed, I strained to look at his face. He looked up. It was too dark to make out his features.

On to railway tracks, across them, past wagons and engines to a platform. The bus stopped; the door opened; Sergei told us to get off. We huddled on the platform, looking across at a group of Russian women. First impression: how poor they looked. Clothes which hung, high boots with heels that laced at the front. Sergei called: 'Come on, let's get on the train.'

A fat woman in a blue nylon coat and white boots held the door open for us. She had a dirty rag in her hand, said hello waving the rag, and dipped her head to us one by one. I walked into the first empty compartment. There were four beds, neatly made with crisp white sheets. Across the window, a lace curtain with a polar motif. I took the bottom right bunk, slung my pack under the bed and sat on the edge. Katherine arrived.

'Any room here?'

'Yeah, step in.'

She took her shoes off, put them next to her bag, asked if she could step on my sheets to get to the bunk above. 'Go ahead,' I said. She had *Gone with the Wind* in her hand.

Next in, two Swedes: Eva and Mariana. 'Mind if we join you?'

'Not at all. Step in.' Baggage pushed under the beds, jackets off, door shut, out with a bottle of wine. We passed the bottle around. Katherine wasn't thirsty. She wanted to read.

Eva and Mariana were midwives. The other Swedes worked in intensive care. Eva told me about Kirkenes hospital, why so many Swedes worked there: the money was good. She was going to stay a year, Mariana for ten months. They asked about me. I told them that after Murmansk I'd probably return to England. No fixed date, but weeks rather than months.

Eva said: 'We're going to have a good time in Murmansk, a really good time.' She opened another bottle of wine.

Sergei popped his head through the door. 'How are you doing?' he asked. 'Comfortable? Settled?'

'Fine, Sergei. Couldn't be better,' said Eva.

He looked at the wine. 'You know,' he said, 'strictly speaking you're not allowed to drink on public transport. It's illegal.'

'Do you want us to put the bottle away?' asked Mariana.

'No, no. Be careful, that's all. Keep the door closed.'

'Would you like some?' asked Eva.

'Sure, why not?' He took the bottle, drank a good mouthful. When he'd gone, Eva said: 'He seems a nice guy.'

We finished the second bottle. Mariana had a third; Bulgarian, did anyone mind?

'No, not at all.'

'Pass it round.'

The woman in the blue coat slid open the door and asked whether we wanted tea. Yes, tea. What a good idea. How many? Four. Four teas.

'You're drunk,' said Katherine.

'How's the book, Katherine?' I asked.

'Not much good,' she said.

'Have a drink,' said Eva.

Katherine sat up and took the bottle. 'It's awful,' she said. 'I need something to eat with this. I've got a bag of grapes in my bag. Anyone want grapes?'

Grapes sounded a good idea. Katherine asked me to find them. I pulled her bag out from under my bed. It contained a book (something by Marge Piercy), a pair of jeans, two pairs of knickers, a Russian phrasebook, a biography of Tolstoy, a pair of socks, a bra.

'Katherine,' I said, 'I can't find the grapes. Where are the grapes?'

'In the plastic bag.'

'Okay. Plastic bag, got you. Here are the grapes, ladies.'

The woman in blue came in with the teas. 'Put them on the table,' I said in Norwegian.

The Swedes liked that. The woman didn't understand a thing. She smiled, gave me a pile of sugar cubes to hold.

Katherine said: 'You're supposed to hold the cubes between your teeth and drink the tea through them.' She'd read that somewhere. I'd seen old men do it in Greece. We tried it, but the cubes crumbled. I spat what was left into the cup and stirred with the corkscrew.

Now that we had tea cups we didn't need to pass the bottle round. Mariana kept us topped up. She was sitting with the bottle when the door crashed open. A soldier looked in, at the beds, at the wine, at the grapes. He slammed the door closed.

That spoilt the party mood. Katherine said she was tired and wanted to sleep. She handed me *Gone with the Wind*, which I put in her knapsack, and she dropped her socks on to the floor. Otherwise she slept fully clothed. Eva and Mariana took it in turns to stand up and undress. I got up to leave, thinking they might want privacy.

Eva said: 'Don't leave for our sake. We're not shy.' She sat topless on her bed while Mariana struggled into a nightdress and then climbed to the bunk above.

I found the light switch, clicked it off and lay listening to the rumbling of the train. A little later, Katherine began snoring: piggy grunts with wheezes between. They kept me awake until Kola, when it was light and I could see dozens of people on the platform, one outside our window – a man with rubber boots and a dog on a string. He had a rifle hanging from his shoulder, and at his feet a full sack. I slept after Kola, not for long because Sergei banged on our door and said Murmansk was the next station. I turned towards the wall, ready to sleep, but was kept awake by Katherine's fidgeting at the end of my bed. She was rummaging through her duffle-bag. Then she left and there was a moment's peace, but she was back within minutes to tell us about the toilet:

'I didn't dare sit on it. There was pee all over the floor.

No toilet paper. The water's brown. The basin's filthy. I'm going to wait until I get to the hotel... Aren't you guys going to get up?' She went out again, 'to look' around.

'She's a bit keen, isn't she,' said Mariana.

Murmansk looked like the Isle of Dogs before redevelopment. 'It's horrible,' said Eva. Shabbily dressed men and women crowded on the platform, their clothes dirty or, at best, the wrong size. The women wore slab shoes: some had fur-topped plastic boots or high lace-up shoes with holes cut for the heel and toes. The men wore suits, lots of checks and stripes, lots of green and brown, and plastic leather-look jackets and coats.

The station building was a green box with a dome on top and above that a rocket-like spire. It might have looked racy in its day. Inside, beneath the dome, were ticket windows, exits for different platforms, and shops and public toilets.

Arne and I needed to pee. We walked along a dim, high-roofed corridor to a huge room with cubicles along the walls. Each cubicle had a hole in the ground, sheets of newspaper on a string and a door that started at knee height. While you stood and peed you could watch men crapping, their trousers around their ankles and balls of excrement hitting the hole and sometimes missing. After that, the men wiped their backsides and dropped the soiled newspaper on to the turds at their feet. A woman with a stick and a bucket went in to poke the turds down the hole and wash the porcelain. She had more than enough to do, rushing from cubicle to cubicle, poking with her stick, answering shouts for more newspaper.

'I hope it's better at the hotel,' said Arne.

Check-in took an hour. Sergei asked us to choose room mates while we waited for our keys. I wanted to ask Mia or Anna, decided I'd settle for Katherine if she asked me. Billy wanted to pay extra for a room on her own. Hugo and Ellen were together. Katarina was Christian's wife, so that solved that. Mariana paired with Eva, Anna with Mia. Mai-Lis asked Katherine. That left me with Arne.

II

After two days in which we had a disappointing tour of a
factory ship and a visit to a deserted polyclinic, there were
complaints from the Swedes. They told Sergei he had a
choice: improve the trips or face a boycott. In response he
offered us a champagne cruise up the Murmansk fjord.

We were locked inside a boat with three crates of champagne and motored up and down for two hours. When the
boat docked in Murmansk we were drunk, seasick and
unable to walk. Which prompted further complaints,
mainly about the hotel food. The buffet restaurant served
the same food for breakfast and lunch: fried fish, sausages,
boiled eggs, grated carrots and black bread. Nor did the
menu vary from day to day.

The Swedes voted to boycott the trips. Sergei called a
meeting. 'I'm sorry, friends, for the circumstances in which
I have to speak. But I must answer the many complaints
I have received. First, food. I propose that we eat in the
main restaurant this evening. There you will be served
caviar, shrimps and beef. Plus champagne and vodka.
Second, the trips. Today I would like you all to visit the
district of Murmansk museum . . .'

'We're not going,' said Christian.

'Please, friends, listen to me. I have arranged for a
specialist to show you round. He is an expert on the history
of Murmansk, and will be able to answer all your questions.
The museum is a fascinating place. I am sure you will

enjoy it. After the visit, I will join you in the restaurant. How does that sound?'

'Excuse us,' said Christian. 'We have to discuss this.' The rest of us waited for the decision.

'Okay,' said Christian after consulting his troops. 'We'll come.'

'Good,' said Sergei. 'I am happy. Now let me introduce you to my colleague, Yuri. He will show you the museum.'

Yuri said: 'Today you will learn about the history of our town and the original inhabitants of Murmansk district, the Sami. You will also be told about the first Arctic expeditions from Murmansk and about the Great Patriotic War. I propose that we walk to the museum; it is only ten minutes from here and the weather today is fine. If you do not wish to accompany the group, you can, of course, go there on your own. It is up to you. I propose to leave in five minutes. If any of you would like to go to your rooms, please do so now.'

Only Katherine decided not to join us. She wanted to go to the cinema. Yuri explained to her where it was and reminded her of our party in the evening. 'Caviar and champagne,' he said, 'so please be there.'

Yuri was older than Sergei but looked in better health. He had black hair parted to the left, short and neatly clipped. He wore a blue suit, a white shirt and a dark blue tie. His shoes were black and highly polished.

Mai-Lis said: 'Looks like they've given us a Party boy.'

Yuri said he liked skiing and shooting. 'I am a sports-man,' he said. 'So please don't expect me to drink very much tonight. We can have a good time without drinking, can't we?'

I think that's what he said. His Norwegian was bad and he spoke in a whisper. When I asked him questions in Danish, he didn't understand. When the Swedes asked him questions, he didn't understand, but I noticed he was more patient with women. He would cock his head, cross his arms and look thoughtfully at the floor. 'Perhaps you would like to say that in English,' he said. 'My English is not perfect, but I understand most words.'

At the museum, he directed us to a box full of slippers. 'Please choose a pair,' he said. 'You tie them around your shoes. They stop you scratching the marble and you help us to keep it polished.'

Mai-Lis thought this was funny; she lined up her friends underneath a painting and got out her camera.

'Do you want to be in the picture, Yuri?' asked Mia.

'I don't like to have my picture taken,' he said.

I had trouble finding slippers big enough to wrap around my walking boots. I took the boots off and left them by the box. I wore the slippers over my socks.

'Your boots will be safe there,' said Yuri. 'I will ensure that nobody moves them.'

The tour started with a talk by the curator, an attractive woman in her thirties. She spoke enthusiastically, looking at our faces as she did so, smiling while Yuri translated. I caught only a fraction of what he said. If he didn't whisper, he mumbled. So I stopped listening and looked at the curator, her cardigan, brown skirt, her tiny high-heeled shoes. Her hair looked like her mother or a friend had cut it: neat, but not quite styled. Her make-up was bright. Her lips shone.

We moved into the Sami room and after the curator's introductory remarks I left the group and looked at the exhibits. There were costumes, pictures of reindeer, Sami household goods such as knives and spoons. There were hunting implements and pictures of Sami huts. An elderly woman was sitting on a chair in a corner of the room and I asked her whether I could take some photographs. She nodded and I took a long time making light readings and setting up my tripod.

Yuri came back into the room as I was packing my gear. 'There you are,' he said. 'I thought we had lost you.'

'Just finishing off,' I said.

'You have a lot of equipment.'

'I like to do it properly.'

'Do you think the pictures will be good?'

'Yes, they will.'

'What will you use them for?'

'For myself. Where are the others?'

'They are resting in the war room.'

'Could I ask you some questions then? About these exhibits.'

'Yes. Will it take long?'

I asked him whether there were still Sami on the Kola peninsula. He said that there were but it was difficult to say exactly how many. Over the years the Sami had mixed with other Arctic races and with Russians. 'In all,' said Yuri, 'there are about 2000 Sami in the Soviet Union. You have to understand that before the revolution conditions were unbearable for the Sami. They were a primitive people. They lived in tents.'

'Perhaps they liked living in tents,' I said.

Yuri doubted whether people would want to live in tents and said that since the revolution modern houses and apartment blocks had been built on the tundra. 'Before Lenin, people on Kola couldn't read or write. They didn't have access to culture and the benefits of city life. Today, Lovozero, the main Sami town, is a thriving town with good housing, a library, the Sami choir, and schools.'

I asked Yuri how reindeer husbandry was organised on Kola.

'Lovozero is the centre for reindeer management. There are four reindeer *sovchos* on Kola, with up to 40,000 reindeer in each *sovchos*. A team of eight people looks after a herd of 3000 animals. In the summer, herds migrate to pasture by the coast. At the beginning of autumn they migrate inland to winter pasture in the woods. Calves are born in May and marked at birth.'

'Do the Sami use snowscooters?'

'Of course. You see they have combined their traditional life with scientific herding. Today they have a choice not to be reindeer herders if they don't want to. In Scandinavia, I know, they have been forced to give up reindeer husbandry. It doesn't pay. Here that isn't the case. We have so much land on Kola.'

I asked whether Sami children were taught in Sami.

'No,' said Yuri. 'They speak Sami at home but in school they are taught in Russian. There are too many Sami dialects. Remember there are only 2000 Sami on Kola, they are not a nationality.'

We moved to the war room where Yuri explained that for forty months between 1941 and 1945, Murmansk was under threat of Nazi occupation. Three-quarters of the town was destroyed but the harbour stayed open and millions of tonnes of food and equipment were shipped to the front. 'Even the Sami played their part,' he said, 'transporting equipment by reindeer sled. And many allied seamen died in Murmansk. They are buried in a military graveyard in the town.'

On to the marine room, where we rejoined the Swedes. They were looking at models of fish and whales. Someone turned the main light off and Yuri asked us to look at the backlit display of plastic cod hanging from strings. He said: 'This is the treasure that makes Murmansk rich.'

III

We were at a table seating eight. I was on a corner next to the dance floor. Opposite me sat Sergei. Next to him was Hugo, and to my left sat Ellen. The first thing we did was to split a bottle of vodka between the four of us, a full glass each. We drank that and ordered champagne. Then a round of beers. Sergei was talking about the dance band. He had a tomato in his mouth; a tomato and a hard-boiled egg. He spat as he spoke. I filled his glass with beer, hoping he would swill down the food before he carried on talking. He didn't. He let the food tumble out of his mouth and scooped it up again with his fingers.

'They play all the hits here,' he said. 'All the latest music. "The Final Countdown", you know. They play that.'

'It's too loud,' I said. 'I can't eat. I can't hear.'

'This is a real party,' he said. 'Loud music, dance music. Good food. Caviar. Vodka. Where's the vodka? Did we finish the vodka?'

'We're drinking beer now.'

'Is it Heineken?'

'Yes.'

'You didn't order Russian beer?'

'No.'

'Good. It tastes of piss.'

'Tell me,' I said, 'where did you learn to speak Norwegian?'

'I wanted to study in Leningrad, at a good school, but

my grades weren't good enough. So I studied Norwegian in Murmansk.'

'Have you ever been to Norway?'

'No. Not yet.'

'Do you want to?'

'Eh, why not?'

Ellen put an arm around my shoulder. She wanted to continue a conversation we had started some time before. 'I was telling you about Albania,' she said. 'I went there last year.'

'And you hated it.'

'When I got there, yes. But I went there with hopes, well, not hopes exactly, expectations. The Soviet Union is a sell-out. Everyone knows that. Same with China. People are too busy trying to look American.'

'And you expected Albania to be different. What was it like?'

'Dull. That was the worst thing about it.'

'Some people say Norway is dull.'

'It is. That's because we're rich, we're lazy. Albania's dull because people have no...freedom. Their lives are decided for them.'

'That shouldn't have been a surprise.'

'I didn't expect cars and nice clothes. Of course not. But passion. Revolutionary spirit.'

'In Albania?'

'Yes. That's what I wanted it to be like.'

'Which countries does that leave? Yugoslavia's out. North Korea's no good. Angola, Mozambique. Not them. Cuba?'

'Cuba! Cuba's finished. Fidel walking around like a soldier, screwing young girls. It's a militarised society.'

'I thought he wore fatigues because he didn't want people saying: "Look, the president's got a smart suit and shiny shoes, and we've got to wear rags and sandals."'

'In the beginning, yes. Now he loves it. So macho, you

know. They love guns and fast cars and American women. All those revolutionaries are the same. I knew a Chilean guy once, a comrade. You know what he wanted me to do?'

'I can imagine.'

'What kind of revolutionary is that?'

'A normal one. How about Nicaragua? Everyone loves Nicaragua.'

'Yeah. Nicaragua seems good for women. I've got hopes for Nicaragua.'

'I wouldn't know. I bet it's just like Cuba.'

'What are you then? Where do you stand?'

'I don't stand anywhere.'

'I don't believe you. When was the last time you did something political?'

'A long time ago. I don't know, when I took my son to a May Day rally in Athens. That was in 1986. The Greek Communist Party.'

'How was it?'

'Boring. Aris didn't enjoy it. Why don't we drink?'

'Good idea. Let's drink to socialism. Hey Hugo...we're drinking to socialism.'

'Is that what it is? It's sad.'

'Why?' I said. 'People are dancing, enjoying themselves.'

'The tourists are dancing. There are no Russians here.'

'Yes, there are. Over by the stairs.'

'They're tarts and their pimps. You want to dance with those women, you've got to pay, preferably in dollars.'

'Who'd want to?' said Ellen.

'Right,' said Hugo. 'The women are awful and the music's lousy. Sorry, Sergei.'

'I don't understand you guys,' said Sergei. 'Those people are talented musicians. They play the music the tourists like. This is a tourist hotel.'

'Why are there no Russians here?'

'You want an honest answer?'

'Of course.'

'We don't want their money. We don't need their money. That's why.'

'With the result that this hotel is like any other hotel. It's not Russian. You give us what you think we want.'

'Western tourists are strange,' said Sergei. 'It's the same in Leningrad, Moscow, anywhere. So many beautiful places to see. And what do the tourists do? They take pictures of queues and rubbish in the street. Why is that? Tell me.'

'Curiosity, that's all,' said Hugo. 'We don't see it at home so we're curious.'

'If I had the money to travel,' said Sergei, 'I wouldn't use it to take pictures of rubbish.'

'Why can't we see both sides of the Soviet Union? What's wrong with that?'

'Do you really expect us to organise trips to the rubbish dumps? Don't be so stupid.'

IV

I gazed across to the nurses' table in front of me. Most of them were dancing: Christian with his wife, the others with a party of Finnish fishermen. Only Anna and Mia were seated, smoking and sipping champagne, picking now and then at a plate of cold cuts. I tried to figure out their ages: somewhere between twenty-five and thirty.

Anna had long fair hair and was dressed in black. She leant back in her chair as she smoked, blowing the smoke up away from Mia and the table. I couldn't see her features clearly but she was unmistakably Scandinavian. Mia could have been Spanish or Italian. She had bushy dark hair and a tan. She reminded me of a Kurdish girlfriend I had lived with some years before; the same thick hair, slim straight nose, large dark eyes.

I looked back at Anna then at Mia again. Mia was the prettier. Anna looked the quieter, more reflective, taking less notice of her dancing friends. She watched the waiters, looked around at the other tables, at the line of women by the stairs. When she had finished her cigarette, she stubbed it out on her dinner plate and half-filled her glass with champagne. She glanced across to where I was sitting and our eyes met. She smiled and raised her hand in a slight wave. I smiled back, lifted my glass. Anna lit another cigarette and turned to speak to Mia.

'Excuse me,' I said to Ellen. 'I'm going to see if one of the nurses wants to dance.'

'Good luck. We'll probably see you on the dance floor.'
I moved tables, sat opposite Anna.

'Hi,' she said.'You're the Englishman, right? I'm Anna.
This is Mia.'

'David,' I said.

'Aren't you dancing?' asked Mia.

'Drinking,' I said, 'With Sergei. I'm having trouble
keeping up.'

'Have one with us,' said Mia. 'We don't drink so fast.'

I poured some champagne. We clinked glasses. Mia
offered me a cigarette. 'No thanks, I don't smoke.'

She took one and tossed the packet on to the table. She
couldn't find her lighter, not in her bag, not among the
plates and glasses, not on the floor. 'Someone's probably
pinched it,' she said and tipped back in her chair, asking a
Finn at the table behind for a light.

He pulled a slim gold lighter from his jacket pocket,
flicked it into flame and made Mia lean forward so that he
could grasp her hands as he lit the cigarette. He asked her
for a dance.

'Of course,' she said.

I filled my glass again and Anna's. 'Skål,' I said.

'Skål.' She leant forward, her elbows resting on the table.
'So,' she said.'What shall we do? Do you want to dance?'

'I'd like to dance.'

We got to the dance floor in time for the last three
numbers: two fast, one slow; all by Stevie Wonder. The
band said thanks. We clapped and clapped, stamped our
feet. No encore. The main lights came on. Anna and I
moved to the stage, sat shoulder to shoulder on the edge,
our feet dangling a few inches from the ground.

'I'm tired,' she said and pressed her head against my
cheek. I could smell her perfume and the scent of shampoo.
'I like your beard,' she said. 'It feels good. You're not going
to shave it off, are you?'

'No.'

'It suits you. Do you always have your hair so short?'

'Yes, now that there isn't so much of it. It would look silly long, wouldn't it? Like that Finnish guy with Mia.'

'Finns,' she said.

'I wonder why they all wear white jackets and shoes.'

'No idea. Men look stupid in white shoes. You haven't got any white shoes, have you?'

'No shoes at all. Just these walking boots.'

'When I first saw you I thought you were an ornithologist.'

'God, no.'

'Or a biologist.'

'No. I don't want to look like a birdwatcher. I thought I looked tough.'

'You don't look tough.'

'What about the beard? It's not a biologist's beard.'

'True.'

'What makes me a biologist? I want to know. I want to get rid of it.'

'Compared with the rest of us, I mean. In Kirkenes we were dressed like we were going on holiday. You looked like you were about to go hitch-hiking.'

'Or birdwatching.'

'Yes.'

'That's terrible.'

'Now I know you're not a birdwatcher, it's okay, isn't it? I don't mind.'

'Did everyone think I looked like that?'

'No. Eva thought you were a schoolteacher. She said you looked sweet, that you were so polite on the train.'

'Come on.'

'Yes. She was looking for you today. I think she's keen.'

'I don't mind that. Does she like schoolteachers?'

'I don't know. Tell me, what do we Swedes look like?'

'Not like nurses. Not like the nurses I'm used to. They're all eighteen with fat legs.'

'In England?'

'Yeah. Student nurses in London.'

'If we don't look like nurses, what then?'

'Something sporting. You could be a badminton team.'

'That's not bad. Not badminton though. You'll have to do better than that.'

'Okay. Skiers. A skiing team. It must be the jackets and training shoes. Only one of you wears dresses, during the day I mean.'

'You think women should wear dresses?'

'Wear what you like.'

'Thanks.'

'It wasn't meant like that.'

'I know . . . And what are you if you're not a biologist?'

'I've done lots of things.'

'You're unemployed?'

'Sort of. I was a journalist. I'm not working now. I've worked as a printer, not actually as a printer. I sold printing work. You understand that? I arranged for printing to be done. I've sold advertising. Wasn't any good at that. I was a student unionist. A few other things. I've worked in a biscuit factory, I've been a proofreader. Some farm work, but not a lot.'

'My father's a farmer.'

'Is he? Thank God I didn't pretend to know about farming.'

'You probably know more than I do. My father didn't like us involved as kids. He said we got in the way.'

'Where's the farm? Where are you from?'

'Småland. Do you know it? In southern Sweden. On the east coast. Near a town called Oskarshamn. What about you? Where do you live?'

'In Greece. Piraeus. That's where I used to live. My wife and children still do.'

'Are you divorced?'

'No. Separated.'

'For how long?'

'Not long. Two months, three months.'

'And you're not going back?'

'I don't know. I miss my son and daughter. They're very young. Perhaps I'll go back.'

'You're just travelling around at the moment? No reason for your trip?'

'It started as a holiday, in Sweden. Now I'm just wandering.'

'Sounds all right.'

'It is . . . Shall we get a drink. I'm thirsty.'

The restaurant was nearly empty. The band had packed away their gear. Waiters and waitresses filled trays with empty glasses and plates and carried them shoulder high to the kitchen. Anna and I sat at our table. The other nurses, and Ellen and Hugo, had left for a party in Eva's room.

Next to us was a table with three Russians; they looked as though they wanted to talk. One had a cigarette between his lips, unlit. His friends were pushing him to ask for a light. He leant over to Anna and made lighter signs with his hand, moving his thumb up and down. She passed him a box of matches which was lying on our table. The men introduced themselves. They lived in Murmansk, were building workers. The cigarette man said he was in the Komsomol. His friends were not Party members. One of them, the shortest, said his father was Greek.

Komsomol man asked where we came from. Anna said Sweden. Sweden didn't interest them. I said London, England. That made them move tables. Now we were five. They asked how long we were going to stay in Murmansk, what we had seen so far, whether we were enjoying ourselves. We said we didn't like the town, the shops were no good, the hotel was no good, and we weren't impressed by the filthy streets. But yes, we were enjoying ourselves.

I asked if they lived far from the hotel. The Greek said he had an apartment about twenty minutes away by car. It was small, but he was lucky to have it. The others lived with their parents. I told them we were tired of being guided around. We wanted to see Murmansk on our own. Why didn't the Greek take us to see his flat? Anna had cigarettes. I had a bottle of vodka and some beer. We could have a party.

It took time to get across what we meant. A lot of sign language and drawing on napkins: a car, an apartment block; five people in the car; an arrow from the car to the apartment; five people sitting round a table drinking, one of them obviously a woman because she had long hair and breasts. The men huddled and deliberated. Anna and I drank our drinks. If they said no, it didn't matter. There was Eva's party upstairs. We didn't expect a yes. From the way the men were waving their arms, we were almost ready to leave.

Komsomol man was spokesman: 'Okay. You come to apartment. You and woman.' I told him her name was Anna. I told him my name too. He said: 'Me, Victor.' The Greek was Alex. The third man was Vassili, or something like it. We called him Vassili.

Alex said: 'We see you five minutes outside hotel.'

'You and woman,' said Vassili.

Victor said we should stay where we were until they had left to get their coats. There was no need to speak to them until we were outside the hotel. When they had gone, I said to Anna: 'Are you happy about this? They seem more interested in you than me.'

'Sure, so long as we stay together.'

A waitress came over and tried to get us to move. She held the back of my chair and started pulling. I told her to go away. She swore at me and called a waiter to help her. He had a waistcoat, black bow tie and hair plastered across his head. He told us to leave. I pocketed the vodka bottle,

Anna carried the beer. Downstairs, we saw Victor queuing for his coat. I walked over to speak to him but he turned his back to me. Anna and I went outside to wait. We stood arm-in-arm by the main entrance, shivering. To our left, one of the Finns was heaving up over the flagstones. His friends were laughing at him.

Victor came out and tapped me on the shoulder. 'Sorry I didn't speak,' he said.

'Where now?' I said.

'Taxi.' We crossed the hotel's square, crossed the road and headed for the Berjoska. We stopped at a group of people waiting on the kerb. Victor told us to stand in the Berjoska's doorway. Alex chatted to a skinny woman in a shiny blue dress. He held her arm, was trying to kiss her, trying to persuade her to come with us. I went over to them and opened my coat showing the vodka bottle. Alex told me to put it away. The woman looked worriedly at me and then at Alex.

He said: 'Tourist.'

The girl smiled at me. I started talking, loudly. She didn't understand. Other people crowded round. A soldier approached. I went over and shook his hand. He bowed his head. I felt someone pulling me from behind.

'Come,' said Victor. He pulled me back to the doorway. Vassili asked whether Anna was my friend or my wife. I said wife. He held both my hands, pointed to my fingers. He made an 'O' with his thumb and index finger.

'No ring,' I said. 'I don't like rings.' Victor explained. Vassili looked doubtful.

I said: 'England. No ring.' Vassili shrugged.

'Where's the taxi?' I asked.

'Moment,' said Victor. 'No problem.'

Vassili was fingering my jacket. I pushed his hand aside. 'Stop it,' I said. Victor understood, snapped at his friend. Vassili muttered a reply.

Alex had stopped a cab and shouted to us to get in. The

driver looked at us and shook his head. He didn't want five
people in his tiny Lada. Victor said Anna and I should go
with Alex. He would come later. The ride was hard and
fast. Alex held up his thumb.

'Okay?' he said. 'You like?'

'Yes,' I said.

We stopped to let some people cross the road. Anna
offered the driver a bottle of beer. He took it without saying
anything, put it under his seat. After a quarter of an hour
he pulled off the main road and took a driveway to a high-
rise block of flats. Alex told him where to stop. I gave the
driver a fistful of notes. It could have been one rouble, it
could have been a hundred. I wasn't thinking. He held out
what I had given him, a crumpled pile in the palm of his
hand.

'Da. Da,' I said. 'Okay.'

'Thank you. Thank you.' He waved as he drove away.
We walked through an underpass into a courtyard with
apartment blocks on all four sides and a low-rise block
in the middle. The high-rise was grey. The low-rise was
coloured – orange or red or brown – in a checkerboard
pattern.

We climbed some stairs to an entrance hall with grey
concrete walls and floor. In one corner was a lift. Alex
pressed a button. He lived on the sixth floor. He rang the
doorbell. A huge man answered: bulging arms, bulging
chest, a thick neck, square jaw. He was wearing a black
T-shirt and jeans. His name: Ivan. We shook hands. Alex
explained that Ivan was a friend, also a builder. He came
over when he wanted to get away from his parents, when
he wanted to drink.

Alex showed me the flat. The tour took thirty seconds.
There was an entrance hall with a cupboard. If you stood
in the middle you could touch all four walls. There was a
toilet and wash basin: you could crap and wash your face
at the same time. He had a kitchen, with room for four

people to sit and no one to move. He had a bedroom, most of which was taken up by a double bed and a wardrobe. In the hall hung a Levis poster, a Rambo poster and a picture of a woman with big tits. One wall of the kitchen was covered with cut-outs from magazines: women's legs, women's breasts, women's faces. Alex and Ivan blew kisses at the wall. In the bedroom, one wall was taken up by a poster of a mountain scene. It shimmered when you looked at it. The bedroom was decorated in purple: purple nylon bedspread, purple carpet, purple wallpaper. The hall was yellow with a brown carpet. The kitchen was cream with brown tiles. In it stood a small table, a cooker, a fridge and a work surface.

Alex sat in a chair near the window and stove. Ivan sat next to the hallway door. I was in between. Anna said she was tired and Alex offered her his bed. When Victor and Vassili arrived, Alex made food: fried eggs, cold fish in batter, sausages, pickled cucumbers. We ate stale bread without butter. We drank tea, vodka and beer. I liked the sausage and the pickles. The fish was oily, had the consistency of fat, not meat.

Ivan wanted to show me a trick. He took a beer bottle, turned it upside down and pressed the cap between his eyebrow and eye. He pushed it in and down, using the bone below his eyebrow as a bottle opener. The bottle hissed open.

Ivan said: 'Me Soviet Rambo.' Then he sprayed the kitchen with make-believe machine-gun fire, and poked me in the chest.

'David. You communist?'

'No,' I said. 'No communist.' Ivan laughed and thumped me on the shoulder. He said, 'Communist,' and spat on the floor. The others laughed.

I pointed at Victor and said, 'Victor, Komsomol.' Ivan said, 'Komsomol,' and spat again on the floor. He looked at Victor and spat at him.

I poked Ivan in the chest and said, 'Anarchist.' He shook his head. What other labels did I know that would make sense in Russian?

'Trotsky,' I said.

'Trotsky, okay,' said Ivan.'Trotsky good.'

I said: 'Nihilist,' and Victor thumped me on the back. Yes, Ivan was a nihilist. Victor made machine-gun noises and threw grenades. 'Nihilist,' he said.

Ivan asked for a pen and paper. Alex fetched a block of plain paper and a biro. Ivan said, 'Communism,' and drew a cartoon of a man in a suit on a lectern. He had his mouth open, speaking. His audience of workers and farmers looked haggard and exhausted. Under the lectern, out of sight of the audience, was a limousine, a roast chicken or duck, sausages, dollars, two women with huge breasts, and a house with columns by the front door. I took the drawing and held it out to Victor.

'Communism?' I asked. He shook his head but didn't speak. Ivan laughed and shook me by the shoulder. 'Communism,' he said.

'Stalinism,' I said.

'Yes,' said Victor and pointed at the picture.

'Brezhnev,' I said. 'Chernenko. Andropov.' I pointed at the picture.

'No, no,' said Ivan. He held out his hand and waved his thumb up and down.

'Andropov,' he said. 'Fifty-fifty.'

'Brezhnev, Chernenko,' I said.

Ivan stood up and doddered as though he were leaning on a walking-stick. I looked at Victor. 'Yes,' he said.

Next question. '*Glasnost*,' I said.

Ivan took the drawing and drew *glasnost* coming out of the speaker's mouth. Standing next to the speaker he drew a woman in a long dress. She had jewels around her neck and on both wrists. She had a tiara in her hair. 'Raisa,' he said.

I pointed at the dress. 'Paris,' I said. Ivan laughed and nodded. He stood up, held his hand to his face and spat on it. '*Glasnost*,' he said and wiped his arse.

'No, no,' said Victor. 'Gorbachev, good man, clever man.'

'Gorbachev,' said Ivan. He knotted his fingers. 'Gorbachev, Brezhnev.' He shook his joined hands in front of me. 'Gorbachev, Brezhnev.'

'Gorbachev, one man,' said Victor. '*Glasnost*, slow! Ten years, twenty years.'

We talked about work. Ivan drew a picture of scaffolding and a man with a hammer and hard hat to show he was a building worker. He said he worked six days a week, every day except Sunday. He worked nine hours a day, was paid 350 roubles a month. What did an English building worker get? I was too drunk to think quickly. I thought of £200 a week, times four. That came to £800 a month. Up it a bit: 1000 roubles a month.

'How many hours?' asked Ivan. I figured forty-five was fair.

'Forty-five,' he said and whistled.

'Saturday, Sunday free,' I said.

'Car?' said Ivan. Did all building workers own a car? I supposed they did.

'Yes, car,' I said.

'Mercedes,' said Ivan.

'No Mercedes. Ford. Toyota. Honda. Fiat. Opel.'

'Lada?' said Victor.

'No Lada,' I said. Ivan spat. He didn't like Ladas.

'House,' said Ivan. 'How much?' I had no idea. I thought of my own mortgage in London for a one-bedroom flat: £100 a week. I said: 'Four hundred roubles a month.'

They whistled. Was I sure? So much? 400 roubles a month! I said I was sure. I asked Alex how much he paid for his flat.

'Twenty-five roubles,' he said. 'Twenty-five roubles a month.'

'Twenty-five roubles,' said Ivan and peered through a tiny hole between his fingers. 'Dog house,' he said.

'How big house in England?' asked Alex. I thought of my flat in London. It was tiny; I couldn't say that most British families lived in something that small. My apartment in Piraeus was the only place I knew the size of. It was big enough for a family of five. I said, 'One hundred and eighty square metres.'

I drew the numbers on a sheet of paper. That much? Was I sure it was that much? 'Family house,' I said. 'Four people, five people.'

'One man, how big?' asked Alex.

I divided 180 by four, had trouble working that out, asked for a bit of paper and told them, 'Forty-five square metres.' They whistled.

I thought I might have exaggerated some of the figures, so I told them there were three million unemployed people in Britain. They couldn't understand that. I tried again. Victor said: 'No work, no money.'

I explained they got money from the government. How much? I didn't know – not a lot. They couldn't understand that people got money for not working. If they can pay you not to work, why not pay you to work? I couldn't answer that by drawing pictures.

I told them I was tired. I noticed that Vassili had gone. Victor and Alex were looking sleepy. Only Ivan wanted to carry on.

He asked, 'You live in England?' I said I did.

'You travel America?' he asked. I explained I hadn't been to America, but I had worked in Greece and Denmark. I thought of other countries and cities that might mean something to them. 'Paris,' I said. 'Berlin. Amsterdam. Zurich. Rome. Warsaw. Belgrade.'

I asked Ivan: 'You travel? Finland? Norway? America?' He drew a picture of a man with huge muscles carrying a suitcase. Underneath the man he wrote 'Soviet'. Around the man and the word, he drew a barbed wire fence.

'No travel,' he said. I took the pen and indicated he could jump over the fence. He shook his head, sprayed me with saliva gun-fire.

I asked Victor if that were true. Could you be shot for trying to leave the country?

'Yes,' he said.

Ivan stood up and held me by both shoulders. He shook me. 'Communism,' he said. 'Communism, no good.'

I told them I had to sleep, had to see how my wife was getting on. Alex held me back.

'No,' he said. I told him I had to sleep. I felt ill, my head was aching. I needed to lie down. Alex said I could sleep in the corridor.

I said: 'Anna. I sleep with Anna.'

'No,' he said. 'No good. Vassili.'

I burst into the bedroom. Vassili leapt naked from the bed. Anna's blouse was undone, her breasts were exposed.

'Okay, okay,' said Vassili holding his underpants over his genitals.

Alex held my arm. 'No noise,' he said. 'Please, no noise. Scandal. Scandal.'

I broke free and rushed over to Anna. She was asleep. 'Wake up,' I said. 'Anna, wake up.'

'I feel terrible,' she said. 'My head feels awful.'

'Did he do anything?' I said. 'Did he do anything to you?'

'Who?'

'The creep who was lying on the bed.'

'Him, is he still here? I told him to go away.'

'Are you okay? He didn't do anything, did he?'

'He tried to undress me.'

'Is that all? Is that all he did?'

'He tried to take my dress off. I told him to stop. He kept trying.'

'Vassili,' I shouted.

'Quiet,' said Alex.

Vassili stood sheepishly in the doorway. 'What the hell do you think you were doing?' I shouted. 'That's my wife.'

'Sorry,' he said. 'I am sorry.'

'Okay,' said Alex. 'Okay.'

'Are you all right, Anna?'

'Yeah, apart from the noise. Can't you tell them to get out? My head hurts.'

Alex brought Vassili and me together, made us shake hands. 'I am sorry,' said Vassili. 'I didn't understand.'

Alex handed me a pair of pyjamas, pointed to his bed. 'Sleep,' he said.

Alex and Vassili left the room. I lay down next to Anna. She said: 'Is that you, David? Is that you?'

'Yes, it's me.'

'Don't leave me. Don't leave me alone with those men. He was playing with himself next to me. I shouted to you. Didn't you hear?'

'I didn't hear a thing. I was in the kitchen telling everybody how much I earned.'

'David? We don't have to make love now, do we? We can make love in Kirkenes, when we get home. Not tonight.'

'Okay. Let's sleep.'

At five in the morning, Alex crawled into the bed with us. We stayed there, the three of us, until seven when I thought it was time to leave. I shook him to say goodbye but he was fast asleep. Anna said she felt terrible. I was fine, tired but not hungover. We left the flat, took the lift to the ground floor and walked out into the courtyard. We found the underpass and walked through to the main road. An old woman was walking towards us.

I said: 'Centrum. Murmansk Centrum.' She pointed in the direction we were heading, to a trolley bus stop. I thanked her and we joined the queue. Half an hour later we were back at the hotel. I saw Anna to her room, went to mine and fell on the bed fully clothed. Arne looked across at me.'That must have been some party you were at.'

'It was,' I said. 'It was.'

'You're not going to get much sleep,' said Arne. 'The train to Nikel leaves in three hours.'

'I'll rest until then.'

'Don't you want any breakfast? I thought we could eat together.'

'I'd like to, but my stomach, I don't think it's up to it.'

'Did you drink a lot?'

'Not a lot exactly. I think it was the food.'

'That's good to hear. I thought I might have missed a decent meal.'

'You didn't. I feel awful.'

'Did you sleep at all last night? I mean did you sleep, you know, anywhere else?'

'No. I was awake all night. I visited a Russian at his flat. He was a nice man. Friendly. We had a few drinks.'

'Really. What did you drink?'

'Vodka mostly.'

'That sounds terribly exciting.'

'I think I'm going to rest now, Arne. I'm sorry to be rude.'

'No, no, that's all right. I'll eat with that Canadian woman, and when it's time to leave I'll wake you up. How does that sound?'

'Sounds fine, Arne. Thanks.'

V

On the train to Nikel, I shared a compartment with Arne, Katherine and Billy. Katherine read *Gone With the Wind*. Billy looked out of the window. Arne tried to teach himself Russian. I tried to sleep. Next door the Swedes were having a party. I could hear their voices and laughter; someone telling a story, the others howling, bottles rolling on the floor. I wanted to join them and talk to Anna but I didn't.

At Nikel, we smiled at each other but sat at opposite ends of the bus to Storskog. When we were asked to get out for a customs inspection, Anna walked past me without a word, without even looking in my direction.

I was the only person who hadn't bought anything in Murmansk. The Swedes had samovars and china and posters of Lenin. Billy had a carrier-bag full of tea and a pair of winter boots. Katherine had an armful of Tolstoy. Hugo and Ellen had a collection of posters, two bottles of champagne and two of vodka. Arne had postcards and a plastic doll.

The customs officers let me through first. Next came Mia. She said, 'How are you feeling?'

'Fine.'

'Anna's ill. Seems like you had . . . what shall I say? An interesting night.'

'We did. Is Anna all right? I haven't spoken to her.'

'I think she's embarrassed. She's not quite sure what

happened. She said you'd be coming with us to Kirkenes, to stay.'

'I'd like to.'

'Good. We've got plenty of room.'

Billy got on the bus and broke up our conversation. She was complaining about the customs officials, saying they were too slow.

Mia said: 'I'll see you later, David. Don't worry about Anna.'

Next on was Katherine, followed by Hugo and Ellen. We waited half an hour for Mai-Lis, Eva, Anna and Mariana to appear. Christian and his wife were still inside the customs hut. Rumour was that they'd been caught for smuggling vodka. Hugo stood up and told some jokes. The best one: Two Sami, Lars and Nils, walking in the forest see one of their friends hanging dead from a tree. Lars says, 'Poor Mikkel. The Lord has taken him.' Nils says, 'Yes, and he used a lassoo.'

An hour later Christian and his wife emerged from the hut. 'Dirty bastards spent an hour and a half looking at Katarina's underwear.'

'Did you have too much drink?' asked Mai-Lis.

''Course not,' said Katarina. 'But they made us empty all our bags. He went through my bras, my knickers, my tampons.'

'The skinny one was a creep,' said Christian. 'You should have seen his eyes. He wanted Katarina to give him a bra.'

Across the border in Storskog, a taxi-bus from Kirkenes was waiting to take us into town. The Swedes lined up to get on. I approached Anna: 'Shall I come with you?' I asked.

'Do you want to?'

'Yes.'

On the bus the driver asked: 'Where to?' Christian said: 'Seven of us to Prestøya.'

Anna shouted: 'Eight.'

'Who's the extra person?' asked Mai-Lis. 'Not the Englishman?'

TEN

Quiet days in Kirkenes

Prestøya is a tiny pear-shaped island two kilometres from Kirkenes. It is connected to the mainland by a road and contains one of Finnmark's two hospitals; the other is at Hammerfest. The nurses and doctors live on the island, in terraced houses which overlook the fjord. Many of them are Swedish and Danish; they come to high-wage Finnmark to save up for cars, a flat or, in Mia's case, an overland journey around the world.

I had intended to spend a couple of days with Anna and then return to England. But at the end of my first week on Prestøya, she asked me to stay another. She showed me cliffs on the mainland where kittiwakes nested, where she had gathered seagulls' eggs to eat for breakfast. She had skied there, she said, and seen fox and hare in their winter coats. We took buckets with us on our walks and collected bilberries and cranberries. Anna had a bottle of vodka at home which she wanted to colour and flavour with cranberry juice.

'You take a half bottle of vodka,' she said, 'and pour it into a 75cl bottle. Then you fill the bottle with berries and leave it for three weeks. After that you strain away the berries and add syrup. Cranberry liqueur, a good Christmas drink.'

We drove to Point 96 in the Pasvik valley, from where you can see the smoke stacks of Nikel and the ever-present sulphur cloud which falls as acid rain on Finnmark. Anna explained that the incidence of cancer was higher in Pasvik than elsewhere in the county of Sør Varanger: 'Doctors think Nikel is responsible. Some days there is more sulphur dioxide in the air than in central Oslo.'

On our way home we stopped at Skafferhullet and looked through the high wire gate on to Boris Gleb power station, a couple of kilometres away in the Soviet Union. If we had wanted to, we could have climbed the gate and crossed the border. Every year a number of people walk into the Soviet Union, many not meaning to. In every case the procedure is the same: the person is picked up by Soviet border guards, questioned and sent back. In Norway there is more questioning and a 1000 kroner fine. 'The border isn't as closed as you might think,' said Anna. 'Reindeer from Norway sometimes wander across it over frozen lakes. Their owners are allowed in by the Soviets to round them up. Wrestlers and skiers from Nikel and Murmansk often compete in Vadsø or Kirkenes. I've seen Russian music groups here.'

Though Norway is a NATO member, the people of Finnmark do not consider the Russians as enemies. The Red Army liberated Finnmark in the autumn of 1944. Soviet soldiers entered Norway near Jarfjord, forcing the German retreat, when the Nazis burnt everything in sight. This is why there are few old buildings in Finnmark.

Anna said she had treated elderly patients whose only topic of conversation was the war. Today, more than forty years later, they still hate to hear German spoken. Some refuse to help when German tourists ask for directions. 'More than 30,000 Norwegians were forcibly evacuated,' she said. 'Some ran away to the hills to avoid being sent south, and spent the winter in unheated cabins, afraid to light fires because they might be seen.'

When we ran out of meat, we drove to Näätämö in Finland, stopping on the way at the Greek Orthodox chapel at Neiden, Norway. Sør Varanger county was part of the

Skolt Sami area. Before the Norwegian–Russian border was fixed in 1826, the Skolt Sami were semi-nomadic, moving between fixed settlements: winter in the forest, summers on the coast. In the spring they fished for salmon in the Neiden river. During the sixteenth century they had been converted to Christianity by the Russian monk Trifon. The chapel at Neiden, Norway's smallest church, is the only obvious evidence of the Skolts in Norway. Like the coast Sami, they have been assimilated, wiped out by Norwegian and Finnish colonisation.

Past Näätämö, north-west of Inari Lake, is a Skolt settlement at Sevettijärvi. In the graveyard, the wooden crosses are inscribed with Russian-sounding names: Fofanoff, Gavriloff, Gerasimoff. These people had been born in Petsamo, now part of the Soviet Union but which had belonged to Finland between 1920 and 1945. After the winter war of 1939–45, the Finns were forced to cede the Petsamo region and the Skolts elected to stay in Finland. The government gave them Sevettijärvi, and provided 51 permanent dwellings for the 276 people who moved there. They were given money to buy reindeer, fishing nets and the right to construct cabins, to collect firewood, to gather hay and lichen for their animals.

We visited the Orthodox church at Sevettijärvi, where I lit a candle for my children and prayed that they were well. We exchanged a couple of words with an old woman wearing a high Skolt bonnet, and drank coffee in the café which overlooks Sevettijärvi lake. While we were sitting there with our half-empty cups, a frail man entered and took a seat across the room. He was brought a tray with dinner, fruit juice and fruit, said thank you softly and ate slowly as though it pained him.

Anna said she had been driving near Sevettijärvi the previous spring, and had found three reindeer skins lying in the road. They were bloody, had meat attached, and the hooves and forelegs hadn't been removed. Thinking she could prepare them herself, she loaded the skins into her car and salted them at home. There they had stayed, neither scraped nor tanned. 'If we pick some bark,' she said, 'we could prepare the skins together. The scraping takes about five hours. Then the pelts have to lie in soapy water for a couple of weeks until the hairs loosen, and then we tan them with bark extract. I'll make you a pair of gloves.'

We collected willow bark from some scrub near Skaffer-hullet, three carrier bags full, and cut it into strips ready to be boiled. The scraping was hard work, pulling away sinews and meat until we had reached the hide. I asked why we couldn't leave the hair on the skins and Anna explained that fur stays on the hide only if the skin has been salted within a few hours of the animal being slaughtered. 'They might have been lying on the road for a long time,' she said.

Working on the skins was a constant reminder that I wouldn't be able to stay in Kirkenes. I was thousands of pounds in debt, which had been building up since my summer cruise on the Hurtigruten.

Anna and I got on so well that I didn't talk of leaving. Her company was a pleasure, always surprising. In England I had grown used to people calling themselves 'Green'. Anna gave meaning to the word, though some of my London friends might have called her cranky. She bought unbleached toilet paper, washing-up liquid without phosphates, organically grown flour. She used recycled paper, returned all her bottles and cans, saved glass jars and yoghurt pots, studied the list of ingredients before buying food.

She enjoyed her work, would come home excited after a hard day. There were cases she called juicy, which meant bloody. They were the best, she said. They tested you, made you think and act quickly. At Kirkenes, she had dealt with Sami who had been stabbed, victims of hunting accidents, children who had drunk paint stripper, a Soviet seaman who had broken his leg: 'He was so happy when we bought him a pair of jeans.' There had been fishermen who had lost fingers and limbs, teenagers close to death after snow-scooter accidents, men suffering from exposure after falling asleep drunk in the snow.

In her free time, Anna liked to walk and ski. She baked bread, picked mushrooms, had a freezer filled with elk meat and venison, which her father had shot and butchered on his Småland farm. She showed me a way of gutting perch which removes skin, head and innards with a couple of incisions and one hard yank. When we were driving back to Kirkenes one night after a trip to Grense Jakobselv, Anna ran over a hare. The animal was badly stunned and its hindlegs looked broken. Anna leapt from the driver's seat, took a rock and hit the animal over the head. She picked it up by the ears and threw it into the boot. 'Dinner,' she said. I gutted it in our kitchen and hung it in the airing cupboard for a couple of days. We ate it with onions and carrots in a red wine sauce.

In my third week, I told Anna I had to leave. If I didn't go back soon, I would be in trouble. Some miserable days followed. We walked, as before, worked on the skins, picked berries, took a last, six-day drive to Karasjok, Kautokeino, Karesuando, Skibotn and Alta, where the car broke down and we had to catch a plane to Kirkenes.

The other nurses who had been to Murmansk organised a farewell party. They cooked borsch, bought vodka and Bull's Blood wine. And when we had drunk enough to talk freely, to sing and dance, Mia said: 'Why don't you work in a fishing factory, David? Lots of foreigners do.'

The others laughed, dismissed the idea. 'Do you know what those places are like?' said Christian, 'with your back to the mountains and your face to the sea?'

'Why not,' said Anna. 'David likes fish.'

ELEVEN

Looking for Mr Fish

I

We drove west along the Varanger fjord; around us, bare, rounded rock, tight folds with birch trees on low ground. At Varangerbotn we headed north along Tana fjord, over treeless tundra to Kongsfjord on the Barents Coast. Between there and Berlevåg, at the top of Varänger-halvøya, we passed silver cliffs to our left and the sea slapping rough to our right. It was a cold, moody October evening. No colour in the landscape and the horizon was indistinct, a blurred line where sky and land merged.

We reached Berlevåg after dark, cruised along the High Street, the only street. Few signs of life: lights behind drawn front room windows, a woman outside the mission house, two boys banging on the grill-bar door. We pulled up next to them, wound down a window and asked about opening times.

'It should have opened half an hour ago,' said one of the boys. The other boy kept banging. A man stuck his head out of an upstairs window, pressing his head and shoulders through the small opening.

'Stop making that noise, for Christ's sake.'

'Get out of bed, Carl.'

'I'll come when I'm ready. Clear off.'

'He's fucking his wife,' said one of the boys to his friend.

Anna asked: 'What's happening?'

'He'll be down in a minute,' said the nearest of the boys. We waited in the car. A light came on at the back of the shop, then at the front and the neon display outside. The man came to the door, took his time to unlock it. The boys were pressed up against the glass, looking in, making faces.

'Come in. Come in,' said Carl. The boys darted for the video counter, began arguing about films.

'You're only allowed children's films,' said Carl. 'No violent stuff.'

'Come on, Carl. Your children's films are rubbish.'

'That's what you can have.' He went to the back of the shop and turned on the grills and chip fryer. He looked up at us and down again. While he was fiddling with the dials, he said: 'Can I help you?'

'Quarter chicken,' I said.

'Two?'

'No,' said Anna. 'Hamburger.'

'French fries or mash?'

'Mash.'

'Anything else?'

'Two cokes.'

'You want the drinks now or you want to wait for the food?'

'We'll take them now.'

'Okay. I'll bring the food to you when it's ready.'

He came to the counter, looked at the boys. 'Haven't you made your minds up yet?'

'We want this one.'

There was an axe on the cover. 'No way.'

'Dad asked us to get this one.'

'Are you sure about that? Do you want me to ring him?'

'He doesn't care.'

'Okay. Take the bloody film. You've got to pay the full price though.' The boys nudged each other, dug into their pockets. One cupped his hands holding the money. The other counted.

'Anything else?' asked Carl, tapping the cash register.

'Packet of Stimorol and two Cokes. Regular.' The boys

Sareks National Park in summer. Crossing a snowfield
north of Unna Stuollo

Jimmy: tired, wet and fed-up

Kebnekaise. View from the East route

Summit of Kebnekaise, 2117 metres above sea level

Party descending Kebnekaise

Tolpagorni, Kebnekaise massif

Birch wood. Summer becoming autumn.

Author in Ellenkoia,
Pasvik National Park,
Norway

Autumn light over Ellenvatnet, Pasvik

Pike and perch caught in Pasvik. Food for a fortnight

Forest reindeer

Wind-dried reindeer carcasses.
Bugøynes, Norway

Author taking a rest on a skiing trip across the Finnmark vidda

Jotkajavri mountain hut, south of Alta on the vidda

Kirkenes in April, showing chimney of Syd Varanger
mining company

Prestøya, Kirkenes, and the Hurtigruten coastal
steamer

left. Carl brought our food to the table. He said: 'Mustard? Ketchup?'

'Please.'

'It's on the counter.'

He pulled a newspaper from the rack and sat at one of the tables reading the front-page story about a child murder in Oslo. 'Do you know about this?' he asked. 'A man in his thirties murdered a young girl and now he wants sympathy because he had an unhappy childhood. Shoot him, I say. Don't tell me he didn't know what he was doing.'

'How long will he be in prison?' I asked.

'Not long enough. He shouldn't be locked up at all. He behaved like an animal, he should be treated like one. Prison's for normal criminals but these kind of people, no amount of prison will help them.'

'Nor hospital,' I said.

'That's right. You can't cure people like that.'

'You don't think so?' said Anna.

'No, I don't,' said Carl.

'That makes you just as bad,' said Anna.

'Crap,' said Carl.

We carried on eating. The chicken wasn't bad but the potatoes were gluey. Anna pushed her plate aside. 'I'll have a coffee instead,' she said. 'Want one?'

'Please.'

'I'll join you,' said Carl. 'Make it three.' He checked the coffee machine. 'Be a couple of minutes, okay?'

'No problem.'

'Where are you people from?' he asked.

'Kirkenes,' said Anna.

'You're not Norwegian.'

'I'm Swedish.'

'And your husband?'

'I'm English,' I said.

'How come you speak Danish?'

'My mother's Danish.'

'So you're not proper English. You're a mixture.'

'A half-breed,' I said.

'Doesn't bother me where you come from so long as you're not black.'

'Why's that?' asked Anna.

'I can't stand them, that's why.'

'You don't see many black people here?'

'You'd be surprised. We've got Tamil refugees in Berlevåg. Too many of them. About eight.'

'Eight's too many?'

'One is too many. You know why Norwegians don't like blacks? Because they refuse to be Norwegian when they come to this country. Got to keep their own food and clothes and language.'

'So what,' I said.

'They can be Tamil at home. I don't care about that. But when they come to my shop, I expect them to speak Norwegian. You're English, right, but you don't expect me to speak English. You're a guest in my country and as long as you understand that, you're welcome.'

'And if I was black?' I said.

'I wouldn't be talking to you ... Here's your coffee. What are you doing in Berlevåg anyway? Are you looking for work?'

'Is there any?'

'Are you looking?'

'I'm looking.'

'And your wife?'

'I'm not his wife. I work in Kirkenes.'

'What are you – nurse? All the foreigners in Kirkenes are nurses.'

'That's right.'

'Nurses are always welcome here. I've got nothing against nurses. What's your name, Englishman?'

'David.'

'Okay, David. Have you worked with fish before?'

'No.'

'Can you fillet fish?'

'No.'

'Are you interested in learning?'

'Yes.'

'You don't sound it.'

'I am. Is there any work?'

'There's always plenty of work. Too much work. Try Ulve. He owns the biggest factory. By the harbour, big white building. Say Carl sent you. Everyone knows me.'

'Is the money good?'

'What do you get in England for cleaning fish?'

'No idea.'

'You don't get nearly as much as in Norway. Ask your wife. She'll tell you. Hey, what's your name?'

'Anna.'

'Okay. Do you get well paid as a nurse?'

'Very well.'

'What do you get? 16,000 kroner a month?'

'More.'

'You see. We're well paid in Norway. Of course you won't get 16,000 at Ulve, maybe half. What's that in pounds?'

'Half 16,000. That's £800 a month.'

'Is that all? Can't be. You'll get more than that. Much more. Speak to Ulve.'

'Today?'

'Whenever you like.'

'When could I start?'

'How do I know? I grill fish. I don't catch them. You know, Anna, you should tell your boyfriend to stop asking so many questions. Offer him work and he wants to know how much he's going to get paid. It's bad manners.'

'It's an important question,' said Anna.

'Sure, but it's not the first he should ask. I don't mind. Couldn't care less. But someone like Ulve might take offence. He's an important man.'

'Mr Fish,' I said.

'That's right,' said Carl. 'Mr Big Fish. You remember that.'

II

There were no lights on at Ulve's and the main door was locked. We walked to the back, by the loading bay and fishing boats: no lights and locked. 'It's Saturday night,' said Anna. 'What do you expect?'

'Carl said...'

'I wouldn't trust him.'

'There're lights on in that trawler. Let's give it a try.' We stood on the quay and shouted. No reply. I jumped on to the deck, tapped on one of the lit windows. No answer. Anna joined me.

'Let's go inside,' she said.

I tapped on the galley door. 'Come in. Come in.' We pushed the door open, stepped in. Two men inside: one in his fifties, one in his thirties. The older man was sitting with a bottle of vodka. He said: 'A woman! Come in and sit down. Lars, get them a beer.'

The younger man went to a small room next door and pulled two beers from a fridge. He opened them with the blade of a pen knife, flicked the tops off so they flew across the room and landed on the table. The old man swept them on to the floor with the back of his hand.

'What can I do for you?' he said. 'What do you want?'

'We're looking for work,' I said.

'Hah. Foreigners looking for work. Do you hear that Ole, they're looking for work.' He kicked something under the table. 'Hey, Ole. We've got guests.' The old man kicked again. Moaning from under the table. 'He's sleeping,' said the old man. 'What kind of work do you want? Are you trawlermen?'

'No. We're looking for Ulve.'

'Hah, Ulve. That bastard. No problem. He's a friend of mine. We'll fix it. Have you worked with fish before?'

'No.'

'Don't worry. Fish is fish. Easy. Come on friends, drink. Drink your beer. Come on. Take some vodka.' He kicked Ole. 'Wake up you lazy bastard, we've got guests.' He kicked him again.

'Stop kicking, you shit,' shouted Ole. 'Kick me again and I'll cut your leg off.'

'Cut my leg off, hah. Come on, try.' He kicked Ole again. And again. 'Cut my leg off. Come on then, try. You've got a knife. Do it.'

The old man screamed, flailed with his arms, knocking bottles off the table. He almost lost the vodka but saved it as it teetered on the table's edge. He screamed again and thrashed with his leg. I thought Christ, Ole's stabbed his leg. Anna gripped my thigh. I looked under the table. Ole had his hands round the old man's ankles. He had his teeth in the old man's shin. The old man was kicking. Ole had him tight, biting hard.

'Stop, for God's sake, Ole, stop,' screamed the old man. He picked a bottle off the table, and poked at Ole's eyes and ears.

Lars, who had been in the little room, said: 'What the hell's going on?'

'Get him off,' shouted the old man. 'Get that crazy bastard off.' Lars went under the table, grabbed a handful of hair and pulled. He had his right forearm around Ole's head, a fistful of hair in his left. He pulled out and up and backed against the wall.

'Sit down, you bastard,' shouted Lars. 'Sit down.'

'Hah,' said the old man, 'Crazy idiot. Bit my fucking leg.

Look.' He put his leg on the table and rolled up the trousers. His shin was bleeding. 'Like a dog,' he said. 'He bit me like a dog. Look, Lars. See the teeth marks? Get some iodine, will you?'

'Idiots,' said Lars.

Ole seemed unconscious on the floor. Anna pulled at my arm and made faces towards Ole. I shrugged.

'Look at him,' said the old man. 'Asleep like a dog.'

'Is he okay?' asked Anna.

'Hah, he's dead. Dead as a herring.'

Anna left the table and crouched beside Ole, placing her hand against his neck. She felt his forehead, rolled him over so he lay on his stomach. 'He's sleeping,' she said.

Lars brought a medical bag. He wiped the old man's leg with a dish cloth and squirted iodine into the wound. 'You want a plaster?'

'No.' The old man rolled down his trouser leg. 'Beer,' he shouted. 'Bring me some beer.' Lars went to the little room, came back with four bottles and opened them with the handle of a fork.

'Put Ole to bed,' said the old man.'I'm sick of looking at him.' I held the door open as Lars dragged Ole out.

'Are you hungry?' asked the old man.

'Yes,' I said.

'Lars will make us some food. What do you want? Eggs? Eggs and steak? Do you eat steak? Good.'

Lars came back. He said: 'Ole's sleeping like a pig.'

'Forget Ole,' said the old man. 'We want food. Eggs and steak.'

'How many eggs do you want?' asked Lars.

'Two,' I said.

'Two,' said Anna.

'Four,' said the old man.

Lars went back to the little room. He nosed around in the fridge, pulling out jars and packets of butter and cheese and put them on the floor until he'd found the steaks. The frying pan was hanging above the fridge, along with a spatula and a saucepan. 'Anyone want peas?' he shouted.

'We don't want peas,' said the old man.

'Turn the TV on,' said Lars. 'Football results.'

'Football,' said the old man. 'Lars, where's my coupon?'

'You put it in your pocket. Your top pocket.'

The old man put the vodka bottle back on the table and kept his hand on it for a while to make sure it had landed safely. He slumped back in his seat and used both hands to get at the top pocket of his shirt. He fumbled with the button. His fingers kept missing the place where they were supposed to be, sliding off the button, down on to his stomach. He stopped, took a breath, tried again, missed the button. 'Bloody shirt,' he said and grabbed the pocket flap, tearing off the button. He reached two fingers into the pocket, pulled out some lumps of paper and fluff. He tossed the papers at me.

'Here,' he said. 'Check the coupon. The results are coming.'

He asked Anna to switch on the TV, which was above her head. The picture was terrible. The old man fiddled with the aerial. It fell off the wall on to the seat. 'Fucking junk,' he said. He tried to fit it back into the slot, but couldn't see; he didn't have his glasses. 'Fix the bloody aerial,' he said to Anna. 'Quick, before the results.'

She couldn't reach.

The old man said: 'Stand on the bloody seat. Come on.'

We didn't have a picture but we had sound: 'And now, today's football results.' The old man threw a pen at me. I marked the results: thirteen in all. He had paid for ten rows. His best one had five correct. He needed at least ten to win any money.

'Come on, tell me. How much have I won?'

Lars, standing in the doorway of the little room, said: 'Nothing. You didn't win anything. You got five.'

'Hah,' said the old man. 'Five. How many did you get?'

'Seven,' said Lars.

'Rubbish,' said the old man. I gave him his coupon. He screwed it up and threw it to the floor. 'Where's the food?'

'Coming,' said Lars.

'Let's drink,' said the old man. He pushed a bottle of beer towards me and filled my glass with vodka. A lot spilled on the table. The old man mopped it up with his hand and sucked his fingers. I made room for the meal by rearranging the bottles on the table into rows.

'Are you thirsty?' asked the old man.

'No,' I said. 'I'm making room.'

'Room? This is how you make room.' He stood up, swept the bottles wildly on to the floor, and on to us. Beer splashed our trousers and jackets.

'Do it,' said the old man. One by one I picked up the bottles which had fallen in my lap and on the seat and dropped them on the floor. They clanked and rolled about.

'What are you playing at?' shouted Lars.

'Tidying up,' I said.

'I don't want bottles on the floor.'

'Have you got a box?' I asked.

'Outside the door.' I stood up, felt like vomiting, and steadied myself against the table and the walls. I lurched through the door, tripping on the raised threshold. I fell on top of the box and lay there.

Lars came out: 'Found it?...What the hell are you doing?'

'I fell over.'

'You're lying on the box.'

'Fuck the box.'

'Clean the bottles up, okay? Stop messing around.'

Anna came out and helped me to my feet. 'I'm ill,' I said.

'I'm not much better. Where's the box?'

'I fell on it. Maybe we can bend it back into shape.' I got to my knees and swayed around trying to get a good grip on the box. I wanted it to stay still but it moved. I tried to bend it. The cardboard tore. 'Bloody box,' I said. I rolled on to my back and kicked it over my head. 'I'm ill,' I said. 'You get the box. I'm going to rest for a while.'

'I'll find another one,' said Anna.

Lars came out again. 'What are you doing?'

I didn't answer. He kicked me in the ribs. 'Are you okay?'

'Just about. Is the food ready?'

'It's been ready for ten minutes. Get up. You'll get cold lying there. Where's your girlfriend?'

'She's looking for a box.'

'Sod the box. We've got plenty of boxes.' He offered a hand and pulled me up.

The old man said: 'Hello, friend. Where have you been? It's dinner time.' On the table were four plates. Lars had eaten his food. The old man was halfway through. I sat next to him.

'You want a beer?' asked Lars.

'Sure,' I said.

'When we've eaten,' said the old man. 'We'll go and find Ulve.'

III

Lars took the empty plates and tossed them into a plastic bowl. The old man said he wanted to change his clothes; he'd be back in a moment. I felt ill. I told Anna I didn't think I'd be able to walk.

'I'll help you,' she said. 'Lean on me.' I stood up and fell back against the wall. I felt vomit rising but swallowed it and stood waiting for the queasiness to pass. Anna stood up and we rested arm-in-arm against the wall. 'We'll be all right,' she said.

The old man came down neatly dressed in a blue shirt and brown jacket. He seemed sober, was steady on his feet, no longer talkative. He climbed nimbly off the boat and waited on the quay as Anna tried to help me up the ladder. 'Stop shoving,' I said. Up on the quay, I tripped on some ropes and fell into a fish tray.

'Mind the ropes,' said the old man.

We walked along the side of Ulve's, on to the main road and crossed it. The old man pointed to a big white house. 'That's Ulve's,' he said. 'That's where you ask for work.'

'Good luck,' said Lars.

Anna and I staggered on to Ulve's lawn. I had to sit down, rest a few minutes.

'Do you think you should ask for a job now? You're drunk. Can't you wait until Monday?'

'I'm not drunk. I don't feel well. It was all those eggs.'

'Get up. Get some air in your lungs. You'll feel better.' I

stood up, stretched, reached down to touch my toes, almost got there and came back up again throwing my hands into the air. I repeated the move. 'Good,' said Anna. 'You're looking good.'

'I feel ready,' I said. I walked up to Ulve's door and banged loudly half a dozen times. No one answered. I banged again.

'Quiet,' said Anna, 'They heard you the first time.'

A girl in her teens opened the door.

'I've come for a job,' I said. 'Tell Ulve I'm here.'

She asked me inside. 'Excuse me,' I said and sat on the stairs.

'Daddy,' the girl shouted. 'There's a man to see you.'

Ulve was upstairs. 'What does he want?'

'Work,' I shouted back. 'I've come for a job – with the fish.'

'It's Saturday night,' bellowed Ulve.

'Don't worry,' I called back. 'I don't want to start until Monday.'

'Sshh,' said the girl, holding a finger over her lips.

'Tell him to go away,' shouted Ulve.

The girl shrugged: 'I'm sorry. It's Saturday, you see. Come to the office on Monday.'

'Thanks,' I said to the girl. 'Thanks,' I shouted up the stairs.

Outside, Anna was sitting on the steps. 'Did you get the job?'

'No job,' I said. 'I've got to come back on Monday.'

'What now?'

'Let's go to the hotel. I feel like dancing.'

IV

The man standing in reception at the Arctic Ocean Hotel had a black moustache and thinning hair combed across his head. He was wearing an oversized white shirt which ballooned at the arms and was gathered at the wrists. Over the shirt he had a maroon waistcoat. He looked like a cabaret act; the sort of man who plays an electric organ.

As we walked past his desk, he said: 'Excuse me. Can I help you?'

'Yes,' I said in English. 'I'm looking for the bar.'

'Straight on, sir.'

I led Anna into a dimly-lit room with soft chairs and low tables. At one end, away from the bar, were tables with napkins and candles. Next to the tables were a dance floor and disco equipment. The bar and restaurant were empty and the disco hadn't started. Anna sat on a sofa not far from the door. I stood at the bar and waited for service . . . No one came, so I called to the man in reception. He looked up from his newspaper, told a woman who was sitting behind him to serve me.

'Two lemonades,' I said.

'No lemonade. I'm sorry.'

'What have you got?'

'We've got Coke. We've got Fanta, and fruit juice.'

'I'll take a Coke and a light beer.' I waited while she poured the drinks.

'I'll bring your drinks to the table.'

'Here,' I said, holding out a 100 Kroner note. 'I'd like to pay.'

'You can pay at your table.'

'I'd like to pay now.' She had served the drinks but didn't take my money until she had tossed the empty bottles into a plastic bin and wiped the counter. I took the drinks with me.

A man in white shoes and slacks and a pink striped shirt came out of a door near reception, popped his head into the bar and looked around: at us, at the chairs, at the drinks display. He was joined by a fat woman wearing a midi-length purple dress and a bald man with a beer gut, wearing a black shirt and a thin white tie. His cream-coloured trousers were too tight at the thighs and a touch too short. The three of them sat at a table next to ours. They chatted a while. The woman wanted to know where the barmaid had gone.

'Maybe she's busy,' said the man in the pink shirt.

Down at the far end, a man in a shiny blue suit was fiddling with the disco equipment. He spun the turntables with his fingers, leafed through the record collection and looked up at his audience.

Anna nudged me and pointed to the door: 'Look, it's Carl. The grill-bar man.'

He was with a dark-haired woman taller than he was and more tastefully dressed. She was wearing a dark blue blouse, black slacks and black high-heeled shoes. Carl had a yellow shirt, white jeans, red socks and white plastic shoes.

'How old do you think he is?' asked Anna,

'Thirty-five,' I said. 'A little older perhaps.'

Carl saw us and shouted across the bar: 'Hello, Englishman. How are you doing?' I said nothing. He joined us at our table. 'So Englishman, did you get a job?'

'Not exactly,' I said. 'I have to try again on Monday.'

'Ulve wasn't in?'

'He was in, but he didn't want to talk to me.'

'Saturday, you see. Don't worry, you'll get work. Take your beautiful friend with you. Ulve won't be able to refuse. Sorry, I've forgotten your name...'

'Anna.'

'Yes, Anna. Anna and...'

'David.'

'Okay. What do you think of Berlevåg? Our little town.'

'I haven't seen anything yet.'

'There's not a lot to see. Only 1300 of us. That's all. What are you drinking, Anna? I see your boyfriend is letting you sit with an empty glass.'

'I'm not thirsty.'

'Nonsense. What'll it be?'

'Nothing. I'm all right, thanks.'

'There's no need to be like that. We're all friends here. You don't mind, do you?'

'No,' I said.

'You see. What are you drinking, David?'

'I'll have a beer.'

'A beer. And for you, Anna, a cocktail, I think.'

'No. Vodka and ice.'

'I like it. I can see that we're going to get on well. Straight vodka, eh.' He couldn't catch the barmaid's eye from our table so he went to the bar, where the woman he had come with was still standing. He ordered the drinks, paid and rejoined us. This time the woman was with him.

'Meet my wife,' he said. 'Hilde.' Anna and I stood up to say hello. 'Sit down for God's sake,' said Carl. 'She's not the queen.' Hilde smiled feebly. The waitress brought the drinks; she wanted to know which drinks went where.

'Just put them on the table,' said Carl. 'I'll sort it out.' First he took the vodka. 'Yours, Anna.' He passed me my beer, took a whisky for himself and then pointed to the last glass on the tray: 'That's yours Hilde. Gin and Seven-up.'

Anna asked Hilde: 'Are you from Berlevåg?'

Carl replied: 'No. I dragged her here. She's from Trondheim. Hates Berlevåg. Don't you, darling?' Hilde smiled. 'Do you know what Berlevåg means?' asked Carl. 'It means Pearl Harbour. You are now sitting in Pearl Harbour. How about that?'

'I'm impressed,' said Anna.

'Impressed. You should be. I was fifteen when I left this town for the first time. You know where I went?'

'Oslo,' I said.

'Very funny. Rio de Janeiro. That's where I went. From Pearl Harbour to Rio. That was a trip, I can tell you. Hilde won't like to hear this but when I came back they had to put me on penicillin for a month.'

My eyes met Hilde's. She looked away.

'It was too much for me,' said Carl. 'From this tiny town to a place where you could buy girls on the street. After a day or so I had things crawling all over my cock and stuff coming out of it. Have you ever had the clap, David?'

'No.'

'I bet you haven't.'

'Did you enjoy yourself?' asked Anna.

'Enjoy myself? I never want that kind of enjoyment again. But it was an experience. We all need them, don't we?'

'Yes,' I said.

'After Rio I saw all kinds of places. Mexico. Panama. Jamaica. The United States. Greenland. Svalbard. All those places, and more.'

'And you came back to Berlevåg,' said Anna.

'Right. I saw the world and came home. I was curious, that's all. You've got to come home some time. The place where you were brought up, maybe it seems a shithole when you're young, but you mature a bit and it doesn't seem so bad. Besides, I knew that my friends were settling down and starting families, building a good life for themselves. I was jealous. What did I have? I'd travelled. But I didn't have a place to live. Didn't have a wife.'

The bar had filled since we had started talking; mostly middle-aged people but some youngsters too. A few of them looked foreign, perhaps from southern Europe.

I wanted another beer and got up to go to the bar. Anna wanted another vodka. Carl asked for a Wolf's Cock.

'I'm not asking for that,' I said.

'Vodka and blackcurrant,' he said.

'Hilde?' She didn't want a drink. She was thinking of going home.

I pushed to the bar and waited for service. The barmaid was talking to a couple of men in suits. When she left them to serve me, they stretched over the bar to look at her legs.

A long-haired man standing next to me said: 'Do you speak English?'

'Yes,' I said.

'I knew you weren't from Berlevåg. Are you looking for work?'

'Yes. At Ulve's.'

'That's where we work, me and my girlfriend. We're from Finland.'

'What's it like?'

'Ulve's? It's shit.'

'I've got to give these drinks to some people,' I said. 'But I'll come back, okay? You can tell me about Ulve.'

'Sure. I'll find Saana-Kaisa. She can tell you too. Her English is better than mine. I'm Marko.'

Back at our table, Carl and Hilde had gone. Anna said Hilde was angry, so the two of them had gone outside to talk. I told her about the Finns. She said: 'Don't leave me alone with Carl for long.'

Marko was standing with a pretty red-haired woman. She looked about eighteen. 'This is Saana-Kaisa.'

'Very pleased to meet you,' she said.

'Hello,' I said. 'I'm David. I'm looking for work at Ulve's.'

Both of them laughed. 'You need work bad?' said Marko.

'I need some money.'

'Are you desperate for money? You've got to be desperate to work for Ulve.'

'Is it that bad?'

Saana-Kaisa said: 'It's terrible. The money is okay but it's not as much as they promise you. You've got to learn first. You get low wages while you're learning...'

'Fifty kroner an hour,' said Marko.

'If you work overtime, you can make a lot,' said Saana-Kaisa. 'But you don't feel like doing it. The work is too hard.'

'We work the minimum,' said Marko. 'Well, I don't work at all. I'm on sick leave.' He had water on the knee from too much standing. 'The secret,' he said, 'is to do something that makes you a little ill. Then you see the doctor. In this country if you've worked for two weeks and you're sick, you get sick money. Better than working, isn't it?'

'Much,' I said. 'Are you sick?'

Marko laughed. 'My knees hurt if I stand up too much. But I could work if I had to. What's the point? You could do the same.'

'I've got a bad back,' I said.

'Perfect. After two weeks you pretend to have an accident. Slip on a fishball. Say it's Ulve's fault. Say you can't work with a bad back.'

'Are you on sick pay?' I asked Saana–Kaisa.

'No. They might be suspicious if we both did it. Maybe later when I've had enough. I get hay fever. I'll say the fish make me sick. Something like that.'

'Tell me about the work,' I said.

'Filleting is the worst work I've done,' said Marko. 'I've worked in theatres carrying lights. I've worked as a roadie. I've worked in construction. I've picked fruit. Filleting is the worst. It stinks. It makes your hair stink, your clothes stink. You come home, you wash your hands, they still stink. You've got a girlfriend, she stinks too.'

'I stink all the time,' said Saana-Kaisa. 'I come home to Marko and he says, 'You smell bad'. We can't sleep together...'

'We do but I don't enjoy it,' said Marko. 'Fish is not good for your sex life.'

'It is if you eat it,' I said.

'You work with fish all day, the last thing you want to do is eat it. Some of the other guys steal a lot. There's a Japanese guy, all he eats is fish. Eats it raw. But not us.'

'The work,' said Saana-Kaisa, 'is non-stop. You have to work like crazy to get the minimum wage. If you are too slow at filleting, they move you to fishballs. It's easier, but more messy. All the rubbish from the fish, all the stuff left over from filleting, goes into the fishball machine.'

'There's loading work too,' said Marko. 'For the men. If you're big like me, they try to get you to load boxes. That's heavy work. I told them, "I look big but I'm weak. I can't load boxes. No way." So they put me on filleting.'

'The easiest job,' said Saana-Kaisa, 'is sweeping the floor. Only a couple of people are lucky enough to do that. They get the basic wage. It's not much, but all they've got to do is sweep up the fish shit.'

'And then they throw it in the fishball machine,' said Marko.

'I don't think I'll try Ulve,' I said.

'Forget fish,' said Marko. 'We do it because we need the money really bad. I can't go back to Finland. They want me to go in the army. Once I've saved money here, I'm going to travel. India or China. I have to do it before my passport runs out. No army service, no passport.'

'What about you, Saana-Kaisa?'

'I don't know. I was a drama student in Helsinki, but I didn't like it. I don't know what I want. We'll stay here for a couple of months. India sounds good.'

'Away from the fucking fish,' said Marko.

'Thanks for warning me,' I said. 'I'd better be getting

back to my girlfriend now. She's sitting with a guy she doesn't like.'

Carl saw me coming. He moved away from Anna, left space between her thigh and his. 'What were we talking about?' he said.

'Your son,' said Anna.

'That's right, the little bastard. Won't do anything I tell him. Sometimes I feel like strangling him. I think he's going to have problems. The only thing he's good at is wrestling. Mad about wrestling.'

'Would you like to dance?' I asked Anna.

'Sure,' she said.

'Excuse us,' I said to Carl.

The disco man was playing Swedish accordion music. We tried to waltz. Anna said: 'Let's go soon. I've had enough. All the time you were away, Carl was touching my knee. He tried to hold my hand. He asked me to go home with him.'

'What did you say?'

'What do you think? Then he started to tell me about his wife, how moody she is, and his son.'

'You didn't have to sit with him.'

'No? I danced a couple of times with some other men. They were just as bad. One tried to kiss me. Another had his hands all over my arse.'

We danced to another couple of accordion songs and a slow song by the Norwegian singer Jørn Hoel. 'Let's go,' said Anna afterwards.

'Okay. I've got to get my jacket first. It's on the sofa.'

'Can you get mine too? I'll see you in reception.'

Carl had bought a fresh round of drinks: beer and vodka; one straight, one with blackcurrant. 'Where's Anna?'

'Toilet. We're going now.'

'What about your drinks? You can drink yours.'

'Okay.'

'Did I upset you? Is Anna all right?'

'She's all right.'

'Have you got any chewing gum, David? My breath stinks from all these cigarettes.'

'No. I haven't.'

'I was talking to Anna about an idea I had. A party. She seemed interested. How about you?'

'I don't think so.'

'I've been speaking to a couple of people, a couple of friends. They'd like to come too. We could go to my place. It's men and women, you know. Three men, three women, if you include my wife. We could get together, have a few drinks, see what happens.'

'See what happens?'

'Yeah. Have a few drinks. Some nice music.'

'We're tired.'

'My wife wouldn't mind. She's like me. She likes a change now and then. Maybe, who knows, maybe she'll like you. Or we could just drink. What do you say?'

'Are you offering me your wife?'

'I didn't say that. But if she wanted to, you know, I wouldn't mind. It'd be good for her. Or, like I say, we could just drink. It depends on you and Anna. The others are willing.'

'What do you want exactly?'

'I don't want anything. There are no plans.'

'Tell you the truth, I'm not keen on orgies.'

'Who's talking about orgies?'

'You were.'

'I didn't say anything about orgies. Did I use the word?'

'No, but you offered me your wife.'

'You know something, I wouldn't let you near my wife. I wouldn't let you look at my wife.'

'That's good.'

'What is?'

'That you love your wife.'

'Don't be cheeky, Englishman.'

'I'm not. I said it's good that you love your wife.'

'What do you know about it?'

'More than you think.'

'You don't know anything. I was fucking before you were born.'

I said in English: 'And you're still a fucker.'

'What was that? What did you say?'

'I said you still like to fuck.'

'What's that supposed to mean?'

'Nothing much.'

'Are you trying to be clever?' He gripped my wrist and breathed into my face. 'Do you think I'm stupid, Englishman? I could kill you with my hands.'

'You're right about your breath,' I said. 'It stinks.' I pushed him away. 'And let go of me.'

'I do what I want in my town. I could kill you. You want me to try?'

'No. I want to sleep.'

I stood up. Carl grabbed my trouser leg. 'Sit down. I haven't finished with you.'

I pulled my leg free. 'Enjoy your party, Carl.'

V

We slept in the car with the back seat folded down. Anna wrapped herself round me, stuck her knee between my legs. She slept well. I didn't. I need room to move.

At 8 am, I pulled free and said: 'Let's go home.'

'Now? Today? What about the job?'

'Sod the job.'

We crawled out of the sleeping bags, opened the hatchback. I got out to pee. Wind was howling around the car, blowing in from the sea. 'I can't work here,' I said. 'What is there? Fish and sex freaks.'

'People talking about sex,' said Anna. She climbed into the driver's seat and opened the passenger seat for me. 'I need a shower,' she said. 'I want to brush my teeth.'

'We'll be in Kirkenes in a few hours. Hot water. Comfortable bed. Good food. Come on. Start the car.'

'Which way is it? I've forgotten.'

'I don't know. Go anywhere. We'll get out eventually.'

'Straight on then.' We drove a few hundred metres. The road stopped at a cliff. To our left was a road leading to a building site. Anna turned in, hoping it might bring us back to the town's main street. But the road ended at a line of barrack-like huts which overlooked scaffolding and the foundations of a building. Anna tried a three-point turn, was almost round when the tires stuck in mud. I got out to push, saw that the front left tire was deep in water.

I pushed and pulled as the engine strained but we stayed there, stuck.

A man in red overalls, clutching his hair to stop it flapping in the wind, shouted from the main hut: 'You need help?'

We said we did. 'Hang on a minute. I'll get some people.' He came out wearing a bobble hat and was followed by three men in overalls. The five of us lined up at the back of the car and when Anna shouted 'Ready', we shoved. And shoved. The tire screeched round, wouldn't grip.

The man in the bobble hat fetched a spade and dug a hole round the submerged wheel. He splashed the water out and filled the hole with gravel. We pushed again. The car lurched forward and out of the hole. Anna drove on to firm ground.

'What are you doing?' asked the man in the hat. 'Have you come to see us?'

'We're trying to get back to town.'

'You're not looking for work then?'

'I'm looking.'

'Do you want building work?'

'Have you got work?'

'Plenty. Unskilled, you know. Are you interested?'

'Sure.'

'Have you done building before?'

'No. I studied it.'

'That won't help much. We need hod carriers, that kind of thing.'

'I can do that.'

'Is that your wife?'

'No. A friend.'

'Is she looking for work?'

'No, she's got a job.'

'You live near here?'

'Kirkenes.'

'Could you move here? Without your girlfriend, I mean.'

'I could do that, yeah. For how long?'

'How long do you want? The men here have got contracts until February.'

'February's fine.'

'You're Danish, aren't you?'

'No. English.'

'Have you got working papers? A residence permit?'

'No.'

'You reckon you could get them?'

'I could try.'

'It's Sunday today. Why don't you start on Thursday. How about that?'

'That's fine.'

'Your'e sure your friend there won't mind.'

'She'll be happy.'

'See you Thursday then ... It's bloody cold out here. You don't want to ask any more, do you?'

'No. Thursday. If I've got any questions ...'

'Ask them then. I'll see you.'

TWELVE

To build a wall

I

On Thursday afternoon, the man who had helped us with the car met me at Berlevåg airport in a minibus. He drove straight to the site, showed me to my room and asked me to join him in his office as soon as I was ready.

'My name's Gunnar,' he said. 'I'm the site engineer, the boss. You won't see much of me during the day because I'm in here. Your day-to-day boss is a man called Leif. He's the young guy, tall with a moustache. We saw him when we came in. He'll tell you what to do. If you've got questions, he'll sort you out. He doesn't talk much, but he's good. What I want you to do, David, is build a wall. I know you haven't built walls before, but this is one no one will see – a wall between walls. Outside you'll find palettes with breeze blocks. Find yourself a wheelbarrow and fill it with blocks. Leif'll show you how I want the bricks laid.'

'Right.'

'Norway's a bureaucratic place, so I don't know how long it's going to take to get your working papers sorted out. Could take a week, could take a month. It's not our fault, so I'm going to let you start work today. Here's your contract. All you've got to do is sign. You can read Norwegian, so I don't need to explain the small print. You get paid by the hour, 72 kroner an hour. You start at seven in the morning and get a ten-minute break at nine. Lunch is at 12.30, you're back on site at one; 3.30's dinner, back on site at four and you work till 7.30. Saturdays, you work till one.'

'That's a long week.'

'We're working to a deadline. If we're not finished by the first of February, the firm's got to pay. So if we get behind, we'll have to work Sundays as well. It's happened before.'

'I understand.'

'Finally: you get a free flight home every three weeks. That doesn't mean London. For you it's Kirkenes. I guess that's all right with you. You've got a woman there. Any questions?'

'What about food?'

'We've got a woman who comes in to cook. She's not much good. If it's not fish she doesn't know what to do with it. But she's better than Ole or any of the others. When you work outside all day, you can eat anything.'

II

First there was the wind blowing in from the sea, blowing slivers of brick in my face and eyes. When the itching got too bad, I took off my padded rubber gloves and poked around in my eye with the nail of my index finger.

Second was the pain; my wrists and back. The wheelbarrow held six blocks. At first I carried two at a time, but then Leif complained, said I could carry six. Every fifteen minutes I wheeled the loaded barrow 50 metres through mud and water.

Third was the cold. The higher I climbed the ladder, the colder it got. When I wheeled the barrow past the wall on to open ground, the wind bit through my canvas overalls. Early morning and late evening I couldn't get any life into my fingers. When it snowed, my ears wanted to fall off.

On the second day, Gunnar asked for a progress report.

I said: 'I've got three problems: wind, pain and cold. I can't do anything about the wind. Like you say, it blows all the time. But I think you could move the palettes closer to the wall. It's a waste of time for me to wheel the wheelbarrow 50 metres every time I need a refill. As for the cold, I notice everyone else has got thick red overalls. Look at mine, car mechanics' overalls. Can't you get me a pair of red ones?'

Gunnar said: 'Where the palettes are located, that's a site problem. You've got to ask Leif about that. It's his responsibility. I don't want to get involved. Overalls: I thought of that the day you joined us and I've sent to head office in Tromsø for a pair. But first they've got to find them, then send them. It takes time. If you're that cold, buy a couple of jumpers. It's October now, meaning it's quite warm. What do you expect it to be like in January?'

Getting up in the morning was no problem. At six o'clock sharp, Leif banged on my door: 'Your turn for the shower.' Breakfast meant porridge made with water, plus bread and jam or bread and cheese, and coffee: strong, black, unsweetened. Lunch was a glass of squash, leftovers from the evening before, usually fish, fried with a couple of eggs; plus bread and cheese or bread and jam, followed by coffee. Dinner was a piece of fish, boiled potatoes, carrots or cabbage, and melted butter for gravy. Dessert was fruit soup. Some days it was strawberry. Others it was raspberry or cherry. After dinner we had coffee. At the end of the day, when we walked in at 7.30, we drank vodka and coffee. If anyone was hungry, they could go to the fridge and butter themselves a jam sandwich. At ten o'clock the workers went to bed.

Gunnar and I were always last to leave the sitting room. We watched TV until closedown – about eleven – then he nipped into his office for a fresh bottle of vodka and we sat drinking. Some nights, he said: 'Fancy a beer?' and we'd wander to the fishermen's bar in a house adjoining the hotel.

Away from the site, Gunnar liked to give me personal advice. One night he said: 'David, I've noticed the way you're getting very friendly with that married woman, Reidun.'

'Friendly, yes.'

'Look, I'm a foreigner like you. I'm from Finland. In places like this, these small fishing villages, foreign men are desirable. When I moved to Norway, I couldn't believe it. The women lined up to be screwed. I'm not saying there's anything wrong with it, but look at my example. I moved to Tromsø while I still had a wife in Finland. And I caught something from one of those Norwegian women. It took time to get rid of it and meanwhile I couldn't do anything with the wife. I had to make out I had a psychological problem. She wanted to make love, I had to say I had a headache or her food was no good, something like that.'

'You're telling me to take precautions?'

'No offence, David. But if a woman is willing to do it with you on the first night then she'll do it with anyone. And these days you've got to be careful. I don't need to talk about AIDS.'

'No, you don't.'

'Save your stuff for your woman in Kirkenes. Three weeks isn't a long time to go without. Don't be tempted by all those fish factory women. Do it to them once and they'll never leave you alone.'

The wall was three-quarters finished. Leif and Ole stood looking at it while I was up the ladder. Ole shouted: 'That's a good wall, David. It's not straight but it's good.'

Leif said: I like the way it sinks in the middle. You see that. The sides are a lot higher than the middle. I'm not criticising, David, just commenting. No one's going to see the wall, so it doesn't matter.'

The phone rang in the office. Leif ran to answer it because Gunnar was in town with one of his lady friends. I climbed down the ladder and started wheeling my wheelbarrow. Ole said: 'I don't know why Leif didn't want to move those palettes. Seems a waste of energy for you to walk all that way to get six blocks. Leif can be funny at times.'

'My back hurts,' I said. 'My fingers hurt. My thumb won't stop bleeding.'

'Your trouble,' said Ole, 'is you're a city boy. You're not

used to working. Give it a couple of months and your hands
will be okay.'

'What about my back?'

'Your back'll be wrecked for good. My back kills me. It's
the same with all the men here. Can't avoid it. By the time
you've finished, your back'll be fucked.'

Leif shouted out of the office window. 'David. Phone
call for you. It's the police.' I dropped the barrow, waded
through mud to the office, wiped my boots and went in.
Leif left me alone.

'Hello,' I said.

'Is that Mr Jones?'

'That's me.'

'It's Vardø police station here. Alien's department. Are
you working at the moment?'

'Not exactly.'

'Have you started work?'

'I haven't actually started.'

'What are you doing?'

'I'm learning.'

'Are you being paid?'

'I don't know.'

'What do you mean, you don't know? Have you signed
a contract?'

'Yes.'

'That means you're working. What were you doing
when I called?'

'I was up a ladder.'

'Doing what?'

'I was carrying some bricks.'

'Right. I want you to stop immediately. I don't want you
to do work of any sort.'

'Why? I've signed a contract.'

'You signed the contract before you had permission to
work. You know it's illegal to look for work in Norway?'

'I didn't look, I was offered. What about the people at

Ulve? There are dozens of foreigners there.'

'The law is very complicated, Mr Jones, and I don't want to go into too many details on the phone, but it's like this. Foreigners are allowed temporary three-month permits from 15 May to 15 October. You can't apply before or after those dates. That's why you can't work. The fifteenth has passed.'

'I understand that. But I've got a contract, a place to live, I've got food here. I'm not costing anyone any money. I'm working, building a hospital. I'm working here because they can't get a Norwegian to do the job.'

'I don't want to argue with you, Mr Jones. The law is the law. There's no room for interpretation. If you want to appeal you can.'

'I do. How long will that take?'

'Up to three months.'

'They'll have built the hospital by then. The job's here, now. Isn't there any way you could give me the permit? Are you telling me definitely I'm not and will not be allowed to work?'

'Not only am I saying that, Mr Jones, I'm telling you you've got to be out of the country by the end of the week.'

'The end of the week?'

'I've got your application in front of me and according to what you've written you've been in Norway for two months and three weeks. Is that correct?'

'I suppose so.'

'In that case, you have a week before you have to leave.'

'Why don't you give me a residence permit then? I can do without the work permit if the law is like you say.'

'Mr Jones, the law states that if you wish to reside in Norway you must submit an application from the country in which you have lived for the past six months. Where did you live before you came here?'

'In Greece.'

'That's where you must apply for a residence permit.

From the Norwegian embassy in Athens. Do you understand?'

'Yes. But I don't live in Greece any more.'

'Where do you live?'

'Nowhere. England, I suppose.'

'In that case you would have to try the embassy in
London. They might be able to tell you what to do.'

'I need time to pack my things. Can I take longer than
a week?'

'No, Mr Jones, you cannot. You must be out of the
country within seven days. You can leave from the airport.'

I called Anna at home. No reply. I called her at work.

'Hi, David. How's the building trade?'

'The police have told me to stop. I've got to leave the
country as soon as I get my passport back.'

'What? They can't make you leave. You're British.'

'So what? I've been here too long. My three months are
nearly up. The arsehole told me to fly from Berlevåg.'

'Won't I see you again?'

'How can you?'

'You can't just leave. Not like this.'

'I'll be back as soon as I can sneak back in, through
Denmark or Sweden. Won't be long.'

'Ignore the policeman. Come to Kirkenes.'

'I can't. They've got my passport.'

'Hell, David. This is crazy. I won't see you again.'

'You will. Of course you will.'

THIRTEEN

Winter work

The beginning of winter, at my parents' house. I calculated I was £4000 in debt. In a letter from Greece, my wife said she needed £2500 immediately and £100 a week after that. I didn't have a job. I didn't know how I was going to pay the money back.

I phoned Nick. He said: 'Are you talking about money again, Dave? You know what you are, you're a breadhead.' Nick works three, maybe four, days a week taking pictures of businessmen. He gets them to stand places where you wouldn't expect businessmen to stand: in the canteen or outside on the forecourt or maybe on a park bench, and then he lies down in the grass with a wide angle lens. He looks right up the businessman's legs, right up the man's nose in an unflattering way, then prints the picture hard, lots of black and white. The art editors pay him £200 a day, plus expenses. They send him to Romford, to Walsall, to Willenhall, to Accrington. He's been to Luton, Port Talbot, to Liverpool, to Coventry. That's a big joke: 'The art editor sent me to Coventry.'

I asked Nick whether he could help me, whether I could develop his films or carry his gear or answer his phone. He said no, he liked to, had to, work alone. He prints his pictures in his bathroom sitting on the toilet seat. He has an ansaphone, and the magazines he works for have their own bike service. So no, I couldn't answer his phone or deliver his pictures.

I tried Mark who works for a big publishing house. I taught him proofreading marks when he was looking for a job as a sub-editor. Maybe he'd return the favour. He said he had no work at the moment, but would pass my name around. I didn't expect anything to come of it, so I signed on with an employment agency which sent me to a firm called Hobarts where I worked in the warehouse filling boxes with spare parts for catering machinery.

The manager said: 'You probably think you're clever. We get a lot of people in here who think they're clever. We know all about the faults of our system. You don't have to tell us. You've just got to do what you're told.' I filled boxes with whisks and washers and bolts. I did it for three days. The pay was £2.80 an hour, ten hours a day. Overtime, after eight hours, we got £3.60 an hour. After the three days I didn't feel like going in.

I phoned Nick and asked him out for a drink. We went to Greenwich, sat by the river drinking, then to an Indian restaurant in Blackheath. When I tried to buy a round of drinks, he said: 'No, Chris told me about your money problems. I don't want to talk about money. I don't want to hear about money. Tell me about Norway. Tell me about the fishing villages and Murmansk.'

So I told him how you could sit in a bar in Berlevåg and on the first day people would say hello to you and that would be that. Next day they'd come over and ask if you were staying or looking for work at the filleting plant. You answered those questions and they went back to their seats and carried on drinking. The third day you had women, middle-aged women, sitting on your lap, nibbling your ear. At midnight, when it was time to go home, one or two of the women asked if you'd like to come home and warm their beds. Meanwhile, their husbands were out in fishing boats.

Nick said: 'The women sit on your lap? They come up to you, they don't know you and they sit on your lap?' I said yes, that's what they did. And Nick said he wondered what he was doing taking pictures of men in suits. 'I'm going to see a friend tomorrow,' he said, 'another photographer. Why don't you come along? He'll love your stories.'

The friend used to be a ballet dancer but when he got old – when he was thirty – he decided to be a photographer. He began by taking ballet pictures and then theatre pictures and ended up doing most of his work for advertising agencies and the ad magazine *Campaign*. When Nick was starting out, before he knew how to use artificial lights, he made a list of the photographers he liked and the *Campaign* man came out on top. Nick found his address in the phone book and wrote him a letter. The man wrote back saying he'd never received such a 'genuine, sincere' letter and invited Nick to his house. He explained how to use artificial lights and some weeks later, when Nick broke his arm after a fight outside his flat, the photographer helped him set up his lights so all Nick had to do was press the shutter.

I listened to this and agreed to meet the man, thinking he might help the friend of a friend. We met in a Korean restaurant near Tottenham Court Road. He said: 'So you're David. You like Scandinavia.' I told him yes, I liked Scandinavia. I told him I'd just returned, that I had walked across the Swedish mountains, that I'd worked near North Cape. Before I could get much further the man said he'd canoed across Sweden with his father, from Gothenburg to Stockholm, and what he liked most were the Swedish girls.

I thought I'd have to listen to his boring old sex story, which I did, and then he told me how he was hired by the *Radio Times* to take pictures of Elvis Presley, how he travelled around the States but didn't get any pictures, had to settle for Roy Orbison. He told another story about a teenage girl he'd met in a hotel in Baton Rouge who had 'inflated tits' and had said to him: 'I'm hot, do you want to do it?' And because they didn't worry about AIDS in those days, they did it and afterwards the girl said: 'I want you out of here by the morning.'

I told the *Campaign* photographer that on the anniversary of Presley's death in 1987 I was sitting in a hotel on the Swedish/Norwegian border. I was setting the scene for him, explaining how a man was selling reindeer meat in the car park and how it was raining and cold, when he jumped in with: 'Did I tell you about the time I covered the Cannes film festival and it was full of uptights and tarts?'

He told us the story, mimicking voices, shouting, waving his arms, knocking over a bottle of *sake*, and then cursed the waitress as she tried to wipe the table. He touched her arm and she backed away. 'Don't be so uptight,' he said and carried on with Cannes until I fidgeted and he snapped: 'Stop looking shifty. They're not going to call the police. What's the matter with you?'

I let him finish his story then suggested that we should pay. He said: 'I know Nick invited you tonight, but it doesn't mean I'm going to pay for you, my boy. When I pay I expect bright conversation and quite frankly you've been dull.'

At home there was a letter from Anna on my bed. It said:'I packed my rucksack today with chocolate and oranges and drove out to Langfjord. I parked the car by a bank of snow and skied into the mountains. It was tiring at first, lots of steep slopes and hard snow, but at the top the view was beautiful. I could see high mountains across the border in the Soviet Union. On the way back I skied along a frozen river through a wood. In a clearing I met a man resting by his snowscooter. He said hello and offered me coffee. We sat on the scooter talking about the hospital and about spring and the best skiing weather which starts in March.'

I re-read the letter, finding things I hadn't seen the first time. I got up and knocked on my brother's door.

'Hi, Pete.'

'Yeah. What do you want?'

'Can I borrow your *Playboy?*'

'No way.'

'Go on. I'll give you a quid.'

'All right. It's in the suitcase in the cupboard...and don't get any stains on it this time.'

I lay and looked at the inflated tits for a while, then fell asleep with the light on. In the morning I got a phone call from a social work magazine. The production editor asked me to come in for a trial – 'nothing too taxing' – and if all went well I could start immediately. The pay? A hundred pounds a day.

The trial consisted of editing two articles: one about AIDS research and another about sexual offenders. I had to write headlines and captions and fit the articles into two double page spreads. It was an hour's work. They gave me all day. At 4.30 the production editor said I should go home. She said: 'Don't think you'll have to work this hard every day. We were a bit stretched today.'

They booked me every day for a week, then a month, then they asked me if I could work five months. Five months sounded a hellish long time but I said yes, knowing that I could leave as soon as I'd had enough.

Anna phoned at least twice a week to tell me about her skiing, her training runs in the hills around Kirkenes: 'It was minus 20 yesterday, cloudless, so cold that there was ice on my eyebrows and hair. The snow was rock hard. I'm up to 15 km a day.'

I asked her to tell me about Kirkenes, what the light was like, were there any people on the streets during the day, were the shopping streets full of snow, was the cinema busy, were the bars full; how did people spend their time now they couldn't go out? She answered all my questions eagerly, filling her accounts with details of how people walked in the snow, slipping, sliding along.

'Night times are best,' said Anna. 'The Aurora's been strong lately, not only green but pink and orange. I walked to the top of Prestøya with Mia. Her sister had just had a baby so we took a bottle of champagne with us. You know what happened? It froze in our glasses.'

Anna asked about the social work magazine and I explained how I'd rewritten a social worker's article about care for terminally ill people. He'd written about a client who had a tumour on his neck. Every time the social worker called to see the man, the tumour was bigger. It got bigger and bigger till the man couldn't hold his head up. It oozed and stank and after four months the client died. The article shook me so much I couldn't go out for lunch.

I told Anna I'd be going to Birmingham at the weekend to watch my team, West Bromwich Albion. I promised to send her a match report; she always seemed interested in my football stories, never cut me short when I was explaining how a player made a move or created space, with the result the football stories got longer and in every letter I wrote there was an account of a West Brom match.

'You're not thinking of staying, are you?' she said.

'No.'

'How much longer do you think you'll be?'

'A couple of months,' I said. 'Three at the most.' I didn't say I had been offered work for five months.

Anna said: 'You've been away too long. You should be here now. You know what you're missing.'

Mark offered me extra work on a motor magazine, evening work and weekend work. It averaged out at £500 a week, more than I'd ever earned before. With that much money, I thought, I could buy a car and drive to Kirkenes. I could work the full five months and have enough to live on for a year. I could send Iliana a couple of thousand too.

The social work magazine was beginning to bore me. But it paid well, so I carried on. I edited articles about abuse of various kinds: sexual, alcohol, drug, physical, mental, racial. I edited news stories about social work conferences, bad housing, elderly people, Asian people, Greeks, Cypriots, Vietnamese, inner-city violence and deprivation. I couldn't understand how the staff could be so passionate about their work. One of the feature writers was an AIDS counsellor in his spare time; another did book reviews for the *New Statesman*. You went for a drink with them, they talked about AIDS and social policy. You asked to borrow the book reviewer's *Guardian* and he'd say: 'Yes, but I want it back when you've finished with it. Please don't do the crossword.' I'd say I wanted it for the football reports and he'd look at me like I'd farted.

Mark was better. He said: 'You've got a chance here to make a killing. You'll be on a grand a week if you keep it up. Teach yourself how to take pictures, I could use you instead of Nick. You could do the words and the pics. You've got that social work crap, that'll lead to better things. You'll be set up nicely. You know, you should never have gone on that trip. How long did it take – five months, six months? You know what it did? It took six years off your working life. Made you less attractive to people offering work. It's time to make up for that now.'

I thought about making £1000 a week, about rewriting abuse stories, taking the train every day through south London, taking pictures of men in suits who sold cars or spare parts for industrial cleaners. I'd have the money, more than I needed, but without my children how would I spend it? When I wasn't working, what could I do? Drink, go to football matches, eat out, go to the cinema, the theatre, concerts . . . Is that what I wanted?

I asked Nick, who used to tour the States taking pictures, why he liked his work. He said: 'It's not the people I'm interested in. Men in suits are men in suits. You meet a hundred, one of them says something worth listening to. The rest want to talk about themselves. But there's still the magic of composing a picture, getting the lines and angles right, getting the man to do something with his hands, getting an expression on his face, getting life into him. Then sitting in the dark-room, printing the picture, the right mixture of blacks and whites. The picture and the man, they're two different things. You look at the picture, you think of success, power, authority. Meet the man and he's a boring old fart who needs a secretary to tell him what day of the week it is.'

More letters arrived from Anna. She said she hadn't heard from me for a couple of weeks. Was anything wrong? She'd returned from a skiing trip to Saariselkä in Finland expecting to find lots of cards and letters but there was none. Again the message: 'You should be here now. If you want to work we can move to Sweden. How about Gällivare or Kiruna?'

February came, I phoned my children. Iliana answered. She said: 'Hello, David. How are you doing?'

I said I was working, that I'd send her some money soon. She said our arrangement was working fine; she hadn't argued with anyone for a couple of months. Family and friends had stopped asking where I was – they didn't talk about me at all. The kids were fine. Aris mentioned Daddy now and then; he'd get the photo album out, the one with our wedding pictures, and say: 'That's Daddy. He doesn't live with us.'

I asked to speak to Aris. He said: 'Hello, this is Aris. Hello, Daddy. How are you?' I told him I was well. I told him I was going to see him soon. I asked him about school, about his friends, whether he'd had a good Christmas. I asked him about his sister. He said: 'Alexandra is a good girl. Alexandra is a big girl.'

I asked whether she could talk and Aris said: 'Yes, she can talk. Alexandra talks all the time.'

Iliana came back on the line. She asked when I was coming to visit. She said I couldn't stay with the family,

I'd have to book into an hotel. That was all right with me. That was what I figured Iliana would say.

She wanted to know when exactly I was going to send the money I owed. 'Every week it grows by £100,' she said. 'It's better to pay bit by bit than let it build up.'

'I don't want to argue, Iliana, but £100 a week sounds a hell of a lot. Are you sure it costs that much to look after the children?'

'It costs more, much more. I'm being fair with you. You're going to have to pay soon or...'

'The lawyers will take over. I know. Give me Aris again, will you?'

'He's playing with Alexandra. Hang on. Who's paying for this call, David?'

'I am.'

'Your poor mother, you mean.'

'Can you get Aris?' I heard Iliana calling: 'Come on, Ari, Daddy wants to say goodbye to you.' Quiet for a moment. Iliana put the receiver down.

'Hello, it's me, Ari.'

'Hello again, Ari. Look after Mummy, okay, and Alexandra.'

'Alexandra's a naughty girl. She took my car.'

'She's only playing with it. It doesn't matter. I'm sure you've got lots of cars.'

'I've got a fire engine and a truck.'

I heard Iliana telling him to say goodbye. 'Okay, Ari,' I said. 'Bye-bye. Give Alexandra a kiss from me.'

'Goodbye, Daddy.'

Iliana on the line: 'Is that all, David?'

'Yes. Bye.'

'Goodbye. Don't forget the money.'

I put the phone down and stood for a while. I thought: 'What're Ari and Alex doing now? Are they talking about me? What am I missing?'

*   *   *

I was beginning to forget my children. It had been nearly a year since I had seen them. How much had they changed? How much of me was left? Pointless questions perhaps – questions without answers. But I knew that I was cheating them by living with my parents and doing work that demanded neither thought nor effort. I needed to move, to return to Samiland, where life is slower but more satisfying, where the sky is big, where each season has its own colours and smells, where you can walk for days and not see a soul, where Anna was waiting . . .

FOURTEEN

Samiland is my home

I remember the wind as I left the plane, the wind blowing strong, whipping up pieces of ice and blowing them across the runway in front of me. I walked towards the terminal building, one of the last to leave the plane, across snow, hard and crusty on the tarmac. I was 10 metres from the building, feeling the sting of the wind, and I smiled. I slowed and looked back at the plane, lit dimly by the airport's lights.

I turned to the building and there was Anna, waiting then coming towards me, not rushing but strolling over the snow. She was wearing boots and jeans, a thick down jacket and a black woollen hat, her hair long underneath.

We hugged out in the cold, stood, arms around each other, holding tight; my face in Anna's hair, tasting snow on my lips. She said I was warm and I hugged her again, pressed close to her cheek. An airport official in blue came out of the building and I kept an eye on him, thinking he might ask us to move. But he smiled, stood and watched us and walked on towards the plane. I said to Anna, 'Let's go,' and we walked in to wait for my baggage.

We drove slowly along icy roads through the town, along the fjord which was white with a thick crust of ice. The sky was heavy, laden with snow, and as we reached Prestøya it opened, letting down light, airy flakes which stuck to the windscreen, not melting but forming a sheet, pushed aside by the wipers.

Snow was piled high against the wall of our house, level with the windows half a metre off the ground. On the doorstep was a layer of fresh powder snow, no footprints, no muddy colours. In the hallway, snow fell from my boots and off my jacket and formed small pools of water. It was hot inside. I felt the warmth, like the heat from an oven when one opened the door.

'Welcome home,' said Anna.

I said: 'This time it's for good.'

I sat on the sofa while Anna prepared a meal and then we faced each other eating, not knowing quite what to say. I told her I was glad to be back. Anna asked if I was tired. I said yes and while she showered I undressed, dropping my clothes on the floor next to our mattresses. I was almost asleep when Anna joined me. I felt a tingling on my back, warmth and softness against me. I didn't move. I didn't think to move. But the warmth spread, to my legs, to my stomach and my groin. I turned on to my back and felt Anna's kisses on my neck and cheeks. I raised my arms, up along her back, along the velvet smear of sweat. We rose and sank together, pushing and gliding apart, face to face, Anna's hair tickling my neck. We kissed and made love and when we finished we slept.

EPILOGUE

Listen to the Sami

Yesterday was my thirtieth birthday. Fourteen months have passed since I returned by plane to Kirkenes. It has been a period of deep and lasting personal change. The most abiding memories are of landscape, weather, and time with Anna.

I remember early spring, shortly after my arrival, when we skied across the *vidda*, my beard and eyebrows thick with ice, night temperatures of minus 20 degrees. During those first couple of weeks I skied badly, falling often, unable to take bends at speed, unable to keep up with Anna.

At the state-owned hut at Mollisjok, between Karasjok and Alta, a Sami man offered words of encouragement: 'You're the second Englishman I've seen on skis. The first was Eddie the Eagle. You're better than him.'

The snow began to melt in May, the grey month, with the last patches of ice disappearing in early June. When the fjord ice had gone, the wading birds and seals came. In the middle of May the midnight sun returned, bringing colour to the hills: bright and strong greens, buds on the birch and willow trees, flowers in the woods and marshes. Hare and fox lost their white winter coats and little by litle became brown and red. Ptarmigan cackled into flight, half white, half brown. Along the Varanger fjord, where the snow melts early, reindeer gathered to graze, no longer having to scratch and nuzzle for food.

The *vidda* Sami migrated north to the coast and islands.
In Kirkenes, people packed away their skis, draped tar-
paulins over their snowscooters. The river ice creaked and
groaned and was suddenly bulldozed forwards by the rush
of meltwater. On the Swedish-Finnish border ice blocks
destroyed cabins, a few people drowned. Some scooter
enthusiasts, more foolish than brave and probably drunk,
took a final run on the Tana river and disappeared through
the thin crust of ice. In the mountains, where the lake ice
was still deep, Anna and I drilled holes with an ice bore
and fished with lures for char. Many hours were spent that
way, sitting on a reindeer skin.

The football season began and men and women in warm
track suits and woolly hats practised on the pitches at
Kirkenes and Bjørnevatn. Nordic skiers, after the months-
long winter season, kept in shape by jogging and road
skiing, in which the skis have wheels. Anna and I ran
every morning before breakfast, between five and eight
kilometres: stride for stride, pushing each other on, breathing in together and out ... as intimate as sex.

In Soldier Bay near Prestøya, men worked evenings and
weekends cleaning and painting their small boats. The
kittiwakes and gulls returned to their nesting cliffs where
they would stay screeching and cawing until the end of
summer.

In July, Anna and I walked and fished in Pasvik, staying in our canoe for ten hours at a time, dead-baiting for
pike. We cooked over a pine log fire, watched reindeer,
waited for bear and elk. We swam in the warm green
water of Lake Ellenvatnet, dozed during the long after-
noons, kept half awake by the swarms of mosquitoes and
flies. Anna was bitten badly. Her back looked like a relief
map, with big yellow bumps that took more than a week
to heal.

I learnt how to use a gun and felt the thrill that hunters
talk about when a shot is good and the animal collapses

dead on to its belly. My first kill, a badger, was made far from Samiland, on a farm in southern Sweden, but it was Samiland that had sharpened my senses sufficiently so that I could wait silently for the animal, hear it padding over leaves and twigs, and then, as it trotted into an oat field, hold the heavy gun steady and aim.

The lower barrel blasted shot into the badger's chest and within seconds I had raced to where it had fallen and stood over its body, trembling with excitement. Not sure that the animal was dead, I prodded its head with a stick, half expecting it to turn and bite my leg. But there was no sign of life. Anna, who had been watching, joined me, gave me a hard slap on the back. She was laughing. Later, at the farm, as we were celebrating the shot over a glass of vodka, her farmer friends congratulated me. The Englishman from Samiland was not so strange and stupid after all.

'You've killed your first animal,' said one of them, as though it was part of growing up. And I knew then that I would later learn to shoot elk at home in the north.

When August came we walked in the forest and picked berries and toadstools. There was darkness after months of light nights; the return of a normal work and sleep routine. In September, as the leaves began to fall and the nights became chilly, we hunted hare and ptarmigan. I made cranberry jelly and fruit juice.

Then the rain came and in October the first snow. In November it settled, growing deeper and deeper and we awaited the onset of the Polar Night; no sun until the middle of January. For three months it would be too dark and cold to go skiing: on the *vidda*, temperatures can drop to 40 degrees below freezing. It is the time, according to popular myth, when Scandinavians commit suicide. We rarely heard of anyone who succeeded, or even tried. If people had problems or worries they seemed to drink them away or fight. At weekends the hospital's casualty unit was kept busy patching up stab wounds. When you asked people what they did during the winter, the inevitable reply was 'Sex'.

Unlike many people we knew, Anna and I didn't keep vodka in the house. In dark moments it is too easy to seek comfort in the bottle. Anna told me of a nurse who had been found dead at the water's edge on Prestøya. Lying next to her was an empty spirit bottle and a jar of pills. She had been in Finnmark only a month; in her first days she had spoken enthusiastically, perhaps too much so, about Norway's quietest corner being the best place to sort out one's personal problems.

For Anna and me, life seemed effortless. During a conversation about a neighbour's compulsive need to work overtime, Anna remarked that neither she nor I worked very hard. But we were never short of money, had trouble spending it. While Anna was on the wards, I wrote and read, developed photographs, tied fishing flies, sharpened my knives, repaired our skis and fishing rods.

I have long since stopped worrying about a career, or work to fit my qualifications. It doesn't bother me that the future will be a patchwork of different jobs: factory worker, photographer, writer, waiter, street cleaner. I tell curious friends that this odd-job existence is common in Samiland. The Sami have been practising the art for hundreds of years. In their case they have been reindeer pastoralists, fishermen, crofters, construction workers, trappers and fur traders, souvenir sellers.

The Finnmark *vidda*, the emotional, cultural and administrative heart of Sami nomadism, has taken on a special significance as a buffer between our satisfying life and all that is bad and wrong farther south. In Kirkenes we see and hear little of businessmen with ambitious plans, we see few tourists and even fewer politicians. Letters from home are the only intrusion, and how frustrating I find them. Friends and family have a way of writing that demands and assumes so much. I feel ashamed to admit to them that England and Greece are forgotten countries. I do not think about them. I do not talk about them.

My replies, my counter-arguments, probably don't sound convincing. Samiland must have made me mentally slow: verbally, I'm an idiot. The best that I can do is to describe my days, honestly, accurately, without exaggeration. Words of comparison, better than, bigger than ... I've forgotten how to use them. To me, it is self-evident that life is better here. My Samiland is quiet, restful; its colours are pleasing to the eye. I no longer have to waste time or energy speaking and explaining, fighting to be heard.

I am escaping, say my friends; I have become too weak for city competitiveness; I am romantic, idealistic. I answer by saying that intimacy with natural surroundings is a fundamental need. It enables me to live honestly, simply. If I remember city life correctly, it was full of excess, too much talk, too much noise, too much idleness and wasted time, too much aggression, too much mental anguish, too many plans and schemes; a lot of restlessness; a lot of travel and trouble and little understanding. There was no passion, no strength of feeling.

Harder to explain is what I have learnt from the Sami. What have they given me that is special? It is nothing to do with their bright costumes or their seemingly exotic way of life. It is nothing to do with sympathy for them as an ethnic minority: I find Sami politics as dull as the big city variety. What fascinates me, I am sure, is the Sami's bond with the wilds. Nature has been strong enough to determine their lives. It has shaped their characters, their language, their work.

As a Londoner, I have gone through hard and sometimes painful times learning to like Samiland. During my lone journey through it, many ideas that I had clung to stubbornly were shaken out of my head and shown to be foolish. I learnt new skills: obvious perhaps; humans are adaptable. But I think my response to landscape goes beyond merely fitting in with new surroundings. I have lost the desire, the need, to return to the urban world. I have chosen to settle in Samiland.

On the way, I experienced moments of extreme or exaggerated sensitivity – possibly brought on by hunger or tiredness – in which the actions of city people, the tourists, angered and upset me. People tossing empty cigarette packets and drink cans by the side of the road, picnickers leaving a bag of rubbish under a rock or bush: their thoughtlessness symbolised lost contact with the natural world. The sight of a wind-blown plastic bag on an otherwise wild mountain can ruin my day. It makes me think that I have discovered Samiland too late. It pushes me to the distressing conclusion that the wild areas of the world are disappearing.

People are so arrogant, so confident of their mastery of nature, that they don't consider the long-term effects of their stupidity. I believe the Sami are different. They know what Samiland can tolerate, what is best for its people, wildlife and land. The Sami can be trusted. This is a gut feeling and I know it is simplistic. I know that there are exceptions, especially among young Sami, many of whom want to be as Norwegian, Swedish or Finnish as their non-Sami classmates and friends. For them, contact with nature is a sign of primitiveness. That is why in Karasjok you can see Sami children dropping crisp packets and sweet wrappers. They have become town dwellers.

But there still exist a pure Samiland and pure Sami. I have felt this many times: hearing Sami people speak, reading their books, visiting their homes. During a *yoik* concert in Neiden, given by the Karasjok singer Mari Boine Persen, I was so moved that afterwards I sat for hours by the Neiden river, looking at the waterfall, the white water, the birch trees on the bank. Mari's *yoik* had evoked the wilds so vividly that it didn't seem right to enjoy them in a concert hall with other people. Her *yoik* was the wind, the ground, the river.

Between songs, Mari spoke of the sea Sami who have all but disappeared from Norway's coast. She talked of the Skolt Sami whose culture had been wiped out in Sør Varanger. She was proud, she said, to be part of a revival, part of the struggle to keep Sámi music alive.

During the evening, three shy Skolt women from Sevettijärvi took the stage. Each sang a short *yoik* that they had learned during their childhood in Petsamo. They were followed by four young Finnish Sami from Angeli. That evening, there was no talk of national boundaries, only Samiland.

All agreed that the concert was a success. The local Press were there, the hall was packed. Stirring words were spoken by the head of the county's arts department. He said that the concert was historic, that all encouragement must be given to Sami musicians. He promised that the county council would support similar concerts in the future.

I wondered whether his words were sincere. I had grown used to mistrusting Norwegians. Many I had spoken to considered the Sami pests or scroungers: they have access to grants, they receive subsidies; they enjoy hunting and fishing privileges; they are better off than ethnic Norwegians. The Sami are, allegedly, work-shy, alcoholic, unreliable. They love to complain. They criticise their country. And in Norway that is a major offence. I have often heard the words: 'If you don't like it, leave.'

Norway is young, still struggling to find an identity. It dislikes, and is envious of, its former rulers, Sweden and Denmark. There are only four million people spread across a country which by European standards is big. Norwegians, for all their international good works, dislike foreigners. They are not welcome in Norway. Foreign languages, foreign customs, dark skins, are all considered threats. And the Sami, though they are an indigenous people, are treated like foreigners. The message to them is clear: 'If you are not like us, you are against us.'

The Sami have lived with this for as long as they have existed. These days, the insults probably don't hurt as much as they used to. The Sami know that abuse is a product of ignorance. And perhaps it's a good sign that Norwegians feel threatened. It shows that the Sami are vocal, that the days are gone when a Sami would rather speak bad Norwegian than his own language, when it was believed that all good ideas came from the south.

We have seen that the Norwegians, Swedes, Finns and Russians can make a mess of Samiland. We know the type of life they represent. It is time to listen to the Sami.

Index